Praise for *Witnessing Gri*

"With Margl's courageously open heart, *Witnessing Grief* offers inspiration and a template for inviting the trauma and loss present in our clients to our coaching conversations. We are reminded that a deeply conscious presence is a most precious coaching tool. Moreover, our presence manifests our core drives, and Margl applies the Enneagram personality model in helping coaches own and understand our particular biases in how we see the world and others – a gift to coaches indeed."

Margaret Moore, *MBA, aka Coach Meg*
Founder/CEO, Wellcoaches Corporation
Founder/Chair, Institute of Coaching

"Margl has gifted the coaching community with her role modeling of authenticity. The courage with which she shares her raw and real emotions in service of the professional development of coaches will make you take a deep breath and listen with your heart. With clear examples of coaching scenarios, she holds up the mirror for coaches to recognize when they are reacting to clients in order to escape their own discomforts rather than being with clients in a way that allows them the space and the dignity to grieve. Cleverly integrating the philosophies of the Enneagram, Margl provides a roadmap for the coach to reflect upon their own deeply rooted, often unconscious, habits and provides pathways to freedom from unconscious coaching."

Erika Jackson, *MCC, NBC-HWC*
Chief Coaching Officer, Wellcoaches

"Motivated by years of coaching and the sudden death of her son, Margl brings her heart, body, and mind into this book on working with grief. She brings together the Enneagram with other theories that are highly useful for growing consciousness in oneself as a coach and wisdom on how to deepen presence with clients. The times we are currently navigating, from cultural bias to planetary crisis, call for all practitioners to evolve their capacities. One cannot escape grief. If you want to be a true ally with your clients, Margl's book will serve you. It is a guide and companion along the way, and I highly recommend it."

Renée Rosario, *LPC*
Core Faculty of The Narrative Enneagram

"In a culture that so often hides from grief, this step-by-step guide to understanding and integrating loss is a refreshing change. It contains insights for all."

Richard M. Ryan
Professor, Institute for Positive Psychology and Education,
Australian Catholic University, North Sydney and
Distinguished Professor, College of Education,
Ewha Women's University, South Korea

"Most of us are less than comfortable when confronted with grief, anger, and other negative emotions and seek to avoid or divert these conversations. Alternatively, we may try to add a positive spin or attempt to fix the situation. Despite being well-intentioned, this is not what the person grieving needs. This work provides very practical tools for improving mindfulness and increasing conscious presence...while also incorporating the Enneagram and its harmonic groups. Although written as a resource for coaches, *Witnessing Grief* is applicable for anyone who deals with other human beings...Margl's courage and vulnerability in sharing her own raw experience with trauma and grief adds value and uniqueness for the reader."

Mary B. Rippon, *MD FACS*
Clinical Assistant Professor,
University of South Carolina, School of Medicine Greenville

"In this daring and pertinent book, Margl speaks with courage, grace, and compassion about grief, loss, and trauma. Her work vulnerably describes the unimaginable suffering of a grieving person and lays out concrete, accessible ways to conceptualize and respond to clients, using well-researched information and knowledge about complicated grief and the Enneagram. This book is a must-read for all mental health workers today — coaches, counselors, and therapists alike. *Witnessing Grief* is beautiful, poignant writing about living and working with grief."

Geriann Fedorowicz, *MSW, LICSW*
Grief Therapist

"In *Witnessing Grief*, Margl aptly provides practical guidance with profound transparency and vulnerability, creating sacred space for safety, intimacy, and healing."

Fran Fisher, *MCC*
Author, *Calling Forth Greatness*

"Margl has written a robust and challenging book about grief. While it's primarily designed for coaches, it also applies to anyone supporting another grieving person. The book is powerful as she shares her own story and those of others. It's challenging in that she asks us to consider how we respond to another person's grief, and how we can provide support without diminishing their experience with positivity, intellectualizing, or substituting a belief system for empathy and listening. She reminds us to pause and reflect and to strive for conscious presence. Combining this approach with the enneagram system and the nine personality types makes this even more effective. This book is a significant resource!"

Peter O'Hanrahan
Faculty Member, the Narrative Enneagram School

"Enneagram enthusiasts will appreciate Margl's skill as she incorporates journal entries, captivating examples from clients, and thoughtful exercises to illustrate coaching strategies with an Enneagram perspective. Margl's dedication to coaching is evident on every page as she extends her encouragement to her fellow coaches to be their best. This book is a brave, inspiring, and generous work."

G. Ibele, *MD*

"Margl guides and teaches you how to witness grief—skillfully written to touch your heart so that you can hold the hearts of your clients. Chock full of real nuggets of life and structured to build your coaching skills to a different dimension."

Dr. Henry Toi
Dean of Research and Development, Global Eduhub
Author, *Think to Thrive – reengineering your mind for growth*

"This book should be every coach's companion, as it moves them to a deeper and more conscious presence. Margl's personal experience of grief and loss evoked a multitude of tender learning moments for me, and I wholeheartedly recommend this treasure trove to everyone."

Thomas Lim
Forbes Coach, Public Service Coach, and Author

"For anyone who works directly with other humans, especially at their most vulnerable, this is essential reading. The invitation is here to hold space, reveal shared humanity with others, and be an actual starting point for dialog—what a gift."

Heidi Huelster
Health Educator in the Saint Paul Public Schools Health Start Clinics, Restorative Practitioner, Host of "Parent Town" podcast, and Mother of three

"Some people know a lot but don't necessarily know how to share it. Others are terrific communicators but sometimes lack substance. Margl is that rare breed who has both immense depth of expertise and extensive skill in communication. This wonderful book is the next best thing to in-person interaction and coaching with her. I urge one and all to read, digest, and apply everything contained within these covers."

Kenneth Tan
Chairman, Singapore Film Society

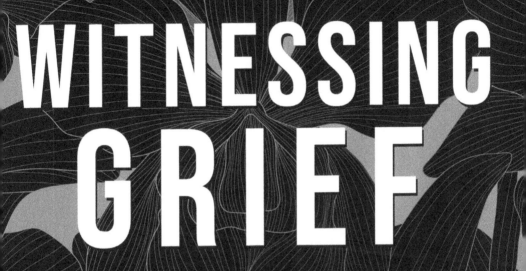

WITNESSING GRIEF

INVITING TRAUMA AND LOSS TO OUR COACHING CONVERSATIONS, AN ENNEAGRAM PERSPECTIVE

HOLLY MARGL

Witnessing Grief: Inviting Trauma and Loss to Our Coaching Conversations, An Enneagram Perspective

www.witnessinggrief.com

Holly Margl, MCC, IEA Accredited Professional, NBCHWC, CSCS

©Copyright 2022

Published by the Compassionate Mind Collaborative.

 CMC

Edited by Heather Doyle Fraser

Cover design by Dino Marino, dinomarino.com

Interior layout and design by Dino Marino

Proofed by Julie Homon

Marketing by Jesse Sussman

Paperback ISBN: 978-1-7372006-7-3

eBook ISBN: 978-1-7372006-8-0

For Benjamin, Joey, and baby Nicholas.

*And in memory of Robert Andrew Margl (1944-2018)
and Nicholas Robert Seidl (1999-2018)*

The world is lackluster without you in it.

TABLE OF CONTENTS

FOREWORD

Love and loss. These words transmit the two most intense conditions that humans can experience. They are the two words that most elicit powerful emotional and archetypal responses in us. Love evokes promise, potential, fulfillment, and connection. We all hope for it, desire it, yearn for it, and pray for it. Yet often, we fear it and push it away in overt, subtle, or unconscious ways. Loss evokes pain, vulnerability, heartbreak, anguish, and separation. We don't want it, wish we didn't experience it, pray that we won't, deny and overlook it, and try to prevent it from causing us pain. Yet loss does happen. It undoes us, cracks us open, and brings us to our knees, even as we pretend or imagine that it has not initiated us into impermanence.

The survival and oldest structures of our brain are still wired for binary discernment. Something is good, so the other is bad…something is desirable, so the other is not…something is us, so the other is not. When this biological tendency is met with a social and cultural landscape that does not readily cultivate depth and presence in human beings, it becomes exceedingly challenging to hold the seemingly disparate qualities of love and loss in the same moment. We think we are either loved or not loved each moment. In the face of unimaginable loss, we feel that love has left our lives.

And therein, the suffering of loss is compounded. When we cannot feel the depth of our grief—when we feel rejected, avoided, disappointed, abandoned, left, or separated by distance or death—we can lose contact with even deeper capacities of our being to love more wildly, completely, and unconditionally. When we can contact the depth of our hearts, it summons forth the potential for abiding and unconditional love through all of the vicissitudes of our human experience.

We are born wired to love. We are wired to love our parents, and perhaps, if this is not thwarted, we will be able to love others, and following that road home, we may come to love everything. Ultimately, love is beyond giving and receiving love. It is about "being love" every moment. For this deeper cultivation to emerge, we need to learn to hold the things in ourselves, others, and life that are seemingly disparate, sometimes confoundingly so. From the binary perspective, we would be unable.

However, there is another orientation that is not binary, not dual – it is triadic, less positional, and opens another dimension. It is a recognition that wherever there are two things, something else is connecting the two views, a possibility that we cannot conceive when we see only from one position or another, take one stance or another, or believe one thing or another. Carl Jung called the development of this capacity "holding the tension of the opposites." George Gurdjieff called it the Law of Three. Essentially, the Law of Three invites us to harness the wisdom and goodness of any two qualities, situations, people, or ideas. Rather than seeing them as opposing, we can clear and release energy from a fixated point of view to see that there's a third force that's connecting the two. This third view arises from the relatedness of the original two in a more sophisticated, differentiated way. By engaging with the energy and wisdom of all three, we now have a vantage point that gives rise to a fourth option – a new emergent and more creative action, choice, or system.

These things are easier said, learned about, and understood than accomplished – particularly in the face of overwhelm, trauma, loss, betrayal, failure, tragedy, and pain beyond the telling. We usually require some invitation, map, design, or support that can assist us in restructuring our orientation from fixation and position to the constantly dynamic flow of learning and loving. The Enneagram is one such offering. It is a brilliant, multi-dimensional map of human potential and consciousness, of non-fixated awareness and being. It guides us in how to release our somatic, emotional, and cognitive energies from protecting ourselves against the fullness of the lifeforce in us and the life around us. These energies can then be utilized for building internal orientations and structures that assist us in becoming fully present and embodying the potential of the life force, presence, love, and wisdom.

The origins and history of the Enneagram are embedded in, as renowned Enneagram teacher Russ Hudson states, "A vast philosophical framework that looks at the nature of the human psyche and its place in a larger cosmos." We find elements of it in Ancient Egypt, Mesopotamia, Judaism, Christianity, Islam, Greek philosophy, Neoplatonism, Hermetic traditions, Jewish Kabala, Sufism, and contemplative Christianity. In modern times, its symbol and overarching meaning were rediscovered and infused into the world by George Gurdjieff, its typology brought forth by Bolivian teacher Oscar Ichazo, and further developed by Chilean psychiatrist Claudio Naranjo. At this point, four teachers arose, each offering seminal and unique understanding and applications for psychological and spiritual development – Helen Palmer, Don Riso, Russ Hudson, and David Daniels. Many others have contributed, including a neuroscience exploration of the Enneagram in a working group with Dan Siegel, David Daniels, Denise Daniels, Jack Killen, and Laura Baker. Its applications are growing, seemingly exponentially, to topics and fields such as parenting, somatic healing and transformation, psychology, religion, education, business, organizational development, community building, DEI (diversity, equity, and inclusion), trauma, music, theater, movies, prison work, social activism, healthcare, breathwork, self-care, policing, and spiritual practices.

The Enneagram describes nine adaptive ways of being in which we over-identify and overuse our natural temperament and gifts to navigate the pain, fear, and challenges of life. Our sense of self, others, and life, and our personal and spiritual development become imbalanced and short-sighted. The Enneagram corresponds precisely to the nine temperaments that psychiatrists Thomas and Chess noted in observing children's behavior and temperament from birth to age twenty-one through the New York Longitudinal Study. It assists us in seeing our natural gifts and tendencies, as well as our constrictions, denials, avoidances, resistance, and fear in bringing forth the fullness of what we are and the protective defenses we have built to guard the precious substance that dwells within.

This precious substance – our gifts and potential, our authentic self – is supported and brought to life in an embodied human experience through our breathing, from the first to the final breath. We are born wired to love, and we are also born wired to breathe. Ancient wisdom and twenty-first-century evidence have now coalesced to show, beyond a shadow of a doubt, that the quality of our breathing is the single most easy, accessible, and powerful thing we can do to change our state and usher us into awareness, mindfulness – presence. Breath is life.

Thus, the shadow of humanity is most transparent and visible in the ways we cause and induce breathlessness… how we overtly, covertly, consciously, unconsciously neglect and cause harm to ourselves, our loved ones, others, other species, and the planet itself. When another person's breath is snuffed out through hatred, marginalization, violence, or othering; when our environment is degraded to the point that makes breathing harder for many; when we lack the will to martial our collective forces to sufficiently address treatment and cures for respiratory illnesses – the shadow of breathlessness is played out. Great dedication, courage, willingness, and love are needed to dissolve these shadows and create a world in which we can all breathe fully. Conscious breathing and Breathwork are emerging as essential medicine.

Loss. How does one bear the loss of a child? With searing honesty and authenticity, Holly Margl lays bare the agony of having her beloved eighteen-year-old son's breath permanently snuffed out by way of an opioid that was maliciously laced with fentanyl. This greed-based insidious use of fentanyl by the drug trade is contributing to a staggering burgeoning tidal wave of breathlessness and death that is wreaking havoc on countless lives through the opioid epidemic and all that has contributed to this unimaginable monster.

How does one carry on when it feels like the most unconditionally living, loving, breathing relationship of our life has been severed by breathlessness? It is compelling to either go into utter despair and collapse – sometimes irreparably, or continually attempt to rise above it. People often do one of these because the onslaught and overwhelm of grief often feel like death while alive. Indeed Holly Margl has visited, and been steeped in, those spaces. These are levels of loss beyond all proportions that arise from a love beyond all proportions.

In addition, whether through luck, insight, wisdom, or grace, she has also found her way to use the wisdom of the Enneagram, as well as the unifying and integrating nature of consciously breathing to engage this hellish-nightmare-initiation into impermanence and liminal space. In a great act of love and service for all of us who love and lose – which is all of us – Holly has offered teachings, practices, and architecture to navigate the unchartered territories each of us takes when loss knocks on our door. She invites us to see how the Enneagram and our breathing help us pay attention to the wealth in grief and loss that we may not have noticed. She invites us to awaken to the ways the love in a situation, place, or relationship lives on to shape us and guide us on remarkable pathways, even when the form of it we knew and appreciated is gone.

In this much-needed book, Holly shares her surrender and goes beyond the binary to a triadic dynamic system through the Enneagram and Breathwork. She opens doors for us to see that which we previously turned a blind (fixated) eye. As the doors begin to open, we can see the views and vistas we had not allowed ourselves in the past. Now we are more able to feel vulnerability, safety, surrender, and flow because of the insight and potential these views offer.

One particularly insightful and innovative offering in this book is Holly's application of the "Harmonics" of the Enneagram, a powerful tool for navigating conflict and challenge that was developed by Russ Hudson, to the wasteland and fiery inferno of loss. Following Holly through these harmonics in the journey of loss creates a more complete alchemy that yields a metamorphosis of the wasteland. In its place, we find an openness, with the fiery inferno burning away the dross of what is not authentic on the pilgrimages into which our losses launch us.

Witnessing Grief is a companion and a practical and inspiring manual. It is not intended to help us "get over something," although something akin to that, yet more true, can happen in working with its methods and practices. It is a guide, friend, arms to cry and scream into, hugs to laugh into, and practicum to traverse each turn of the journey of love-loss-grief-loss-love into living material. And Holly Margl is a uniquely qualified

Sherpa and friend. Judaism teaches that there is no greater loss than the loss of a child. And yet Holly rises up to offer us a substantive hand for all our disappointments and grief – whatever degree, and the shock of loss.

I have yearned for the wisdom of the Enneagram and Breathwork to transform all of our consciousness, spiritual and human potential lineages, and practices. I tremble as I share that I, too, have been inducted early in my life into the undertow of incomprehensible losses of my two beloved younger siblings and my husband, the father of my son. Without reservation, I can say that *Witnessing Grief* is a powerful and seminal contribution to the Enneagram field, to conscious breathing, and to the literature and methods for working with grief.

In this book, we have a confluence of Holly's personal journey with loss and grief, the objective, compassionate, and nuanced guidance of the Enneagram, and the living power of presence in consciously breathing with all three centers of intelligence – body, heart, and head. *Witnessing Grief* can serve as a potent pathway for navigating that awesome, terrifying, and potentially character and wisdom-building territory of the unbearable lightness of being. I am thrilled to the marrow to witness how this book so aptly brings kindness, encouragement, and wisdom to the desert, bottom of the ocean, subterranean caverns, and wildernesses of our bodies, psyches, and souls, so that loss can become a consummation. It can spur love and growth into the love that loss can give rise to if we can travel the tumultuous, uncertain, and life-giving tidal waves of the awareness that every moment and breath is precious.

Jessica Dibb

Inspiration Consciousness School
Spiritual Director and Principal Teacher

Jessica Dibb is a long-time lover, teacher, and innovator of the Enneagram. Throughout, she has been devoted to elevating the teachings of the Enneagram, above the fascination with the Enneagram of personality that has arisen in modern times, to align its teachings and delivery to its original purpose. Its true aim is to show us how – because of fear and the pain of the original wound of separation from the primordial life force and the love within – we delude ourselves into overusing one particular point of view of reality, overusing the gifts of our natural temperament to conscribe us to one primary way of being and miss the totality of who we are.

Jessica founded and is the host of the Shift Network's Annual Enneagram Global Summit and has avidly searched for innovative and useful applications of the Enneagram for embodied, integrated living, and transformation. She also has the joy of being an even longer-lover of Breath and Breathwork, a Breathwork trainer, and the Co-director of the Global Professional Breathwork Alliance. She is currently writing a book on Breathwork, Psychotherapy, and Consciousness.

INTRODUCTION

This book came about because grief and trauma arrived on my doorstep uninvited and with a force so strong that I still have not entirely picked myself up. Indeed, existence becomes surreal when you think about reality, and your mind rejects it.

After my losses in 2018, I learned quickly that most people do not know how to talk about traumatic loss and grief. Without a doubt, niceties and platitudes saturate our society and our conversations. Asking, "How are you?" is commonplace. However, it is extraordinary when the question is genuine. Unfortunately, some semblance of "fine," "good," or "all right" is the expectation, even when none of those are true.

On more than one occasion, people have said that my communication style is direct, so when I chose to answer "how are you" with the truth after experiencing unimaginable trauma, people seemed shocked. But should someone who dreads waking up in the morning fake it so everyone else stays comfortable?

Sadly, through experience and observation, I found that even coaches, counselors, and therapists can say unhelpful and even harmful things. For example, I will say right up front that it is inappropriate to ask someone, "how did they die?" That is an inquiry solely to assuage the questioner's curiosity. This question is not asked with the griever in mind.

Which brings us to an interesting point—how do we know if we are doing or saying something for ourselves or the other person?

This bit of self-insight is where I divide coaches (professionals) from everyone else. When Covid hit, the emotional defense mechanisms I experienced after trauma went viral right in front of my eyes, and "I'm sorry for your loss" became cliché.

The fantastic news is that coaches are the most approachable, supportive, and compassionate folks I know. And most of those I've met are hungry for tips and strategies for talking about grief and trauma with their clients. Undoubtedly, most coaches don't choose this field anticipating such weighty topics. Still, here we are in the Covid era, and along with anxiety and depression, grief and trauma are customary topics of coaching conversations.

So, while this book came about to support my fellow coaches in tackling these complicated subjects, everyone is welcome here.

WHY THE ENNEAGRAM IS INCLUDED IN THIS BOOK

The Enneagram (pronounced ANY-a-gram) is a remarkably dynamic and accurate map of the human psyche, and that's why I've included it in my book. Nevertheless, I'll say a bit more now, and you can learn more later, in chapters four through seven.

The Enneagram dates back thousands of years as a tool for finding our true nature. One cannot pigeonhole the Enneagram as a spiritual or psychological tool; instead, it's both. Humans utilize patterns and habits to navigate life. However, these habits and patterns make life more predictable and keep us from paying attention to what we're doing or experiencing. Fortunately, the Enneagram helps us find and stay with the present moment.

I've veered from the Enneagram's customary presentation in hopes of softening the often rigid hold of "type." It seems too easy to become attached to or avoid a label or title and overlook the motivation behind patterned behaviors. So, as the Enneagram masterly reveals where we mindlessly over-focus our attention, I address that. As you will see, I use *dominant bias* to depict the primary focus of attention for each of the nine numbers on the Enneagram diagram rather than "type" or "point."

The Enneagram is many-layered and nuanced, so we will only scratch the surface in this book. Nonetheless, you will learn more about yourself and how that translates into more courageous and authentic coaching. For once you see yourself with more clarity, you can be present for topics like grief, trauma, and loss with others.

Fair warning, we will not learn about the Enneagram to unravel our clients or loved ones. *The Enneagram is a mirror, not a microscope.*

HOW TO USE THIS BOOK

This book is divided into three parts. *Part I: Meeting Grief* defines and examines grief and how we navigate its path in our lives, and how we may begin to understand how to navigate that path with our clients.

Part II: Using the Enneagram gives a broad overview of the Enneagram and its nine dominant biases. Additionally, these chapters look at how we can use the wisdom of the Enneagram to look at ourselves and the lens with which we view the world. This introspection will allow us to serve our clients more deeply and create a safe space for them as they navigate the complex waters of loss, trauma, and grief.

Part III: Putting It in Action takes everything we've learned in Parts I and II and gives you the opportunity to apply that information to real-life scenarios and coaching situations.

Additionally, each chapter contains specific elements to further your experience as a reader and your understanding of the concepts presented.

CHAPTER-OPENING QUOTES

You'll find quotes from people in my life and both fiction and non-fiction books to support and enhance the content in each chapter and as an expanded understanding of grief's impact on our lives.

CONSIDER THIS AND PAUSE AND REFLECT

"Consider This" passages are active. In other words, these are for more than passive reading—they're for your active consideration, so I ask that you bring mindful attention to the content presented here.

"Pause and Reflect" passages require you to slow your pace and bring a conscious presence to these topics. This content requires inquiry or contemplation with great intention.

GENUINE STORIES AND NARRATIVES

The stories in this book are real accounts. So please hold this thought as you reflect on the people whose lives I've included here. Be aware, however, that for anonymity and confidentiality, modifications may exist.

Chapter 9 includes several coach/client scenarios to help further your understanding and application of the concepts presented in Parts I and II.

You'll find a presenting topic stated in the client's words in each example. Next, you'll find a typical coach response followed by a potential revision to that response that would be more helpful to the client in their distress.

Finally, this book is for coaches; consequently, coaching standards are essential for coaching proficiency. Therefore, each potential revision statement is connected to the International Coaching Federation (ICF) Coaching Competencies demonstrated in the coach/client exchange.

LIVING WITH GRIEF

To get a sense of the rawness of grief and trauma, I've included excerpts from blogs written in the days and months after my son, Nicholas, died. You'll hear a grieving mother's in-the-moment desperate cries for a do-over while rejecting reality. These are my first-hand invitation to witness a mind trying to confront the inconceivable.

CLOSING INQUIRIES

Questions intended to help you think outside the box you've built around yourself. They are to challenge your status quo and expand your awareness of the chapter's topic.

CHAPTER-ENDING QUOTES

These quotes offer different perspectives, either with beneficial information or narrative introspection like the chapter-opening quotes. All of the quotations chosen for this book are to broaden your understanding, sense, and feelings about grief, trauma, and loss.

MY HOPE FOR YOU
AND WHAT YOU WILL EXPERIENCE

First, I want this book to widen your lens of experiences encompassing grief, trauma, and loss so that they become less feared. We'll explore the definitions of grief, trauma, and loss and several *being* coaching skills. Grief encompasses more topics than we might realize, so we're going to take a candid look at where it hides. And we're going to jump right in with a formidable story in Chapter 1 to prime you for learning how to stay present no matter what. As the title suggests, witnessing is a critical factor with heavy coaching topics like grief, trauma, and loss, so we will explore what witnessing means in the coaching venue.

Second, I hope you learn to discern your client from their story and feel confident to bear witness to their suffering. By digging beneath your ego defenses, you can see your patterned emotional reactions in action and how they directly impact your coaching interactions. Without awareness, we hear and see the narratives and often forget about the person telling them. Accordingly, we must know ourselves well enough to recognize where we focus our attention. Thus, we'll use several tools, including the Enneagram and numerous coaching scenarios, to practice noticing where your attention goes with complex narratives.

Third, I hope you discover the fortitude to *be* with and the receptivity to learn from your grieving and traumatized clients. While training and education are vital for masterful coaching, the skill most needed by grieving and traumatized clients is your *being*. Learning to **be** involves inner witnessing and receiving mirroring from others, including our clients. However, humans most often dismiss *being* while over*doing*. And yet, *being* allows for receptivity (letting your guard down) rather than protection (which requires more *doing*). To be sure, your clients feel the difference in your presence.

Finally, when you finish reading this book, I hope you have what you were looking for and feel better prepared to meet your client's as well as your own grief, trauma, and loss.

Holly Margl, MCC, IEA Accredited Professional, NBCHWC, CSCS

"At a broader social level, an understanding of Posttraumatic Growth will produce a greater respect for people who have endured traumatic events. They will be appreciated as people who have been on the hero's journey and have something to offer the rest of us who only dimly perceive what they clearly see."

— Richard G Tedeschi, Jane Shakespeare-Finch,
Kanako Taku, Lawrence G. Calhoun,
Posttraumatic Growth, Theory, Research, and Applications

"They [those having experienced Posttraumatic Growth] can challenge the status quo, build social movements, and ultimately change societies."

— Richard G Tedeschi, Jane Shakespeare-Finch,
Kanako Taku, Lawrence G. Calhoun,
Posttraumatic Growth, Theory, Research, and Applications

PART 1

MEETING GRIEF

CHAPTER ONE

CONSCIOUS PRESENCE

"This pain was like nothing she'd ever known; it was new and terrible.
It was a mother's pain at seeing her precious child destroyed.
And Fiona realized that for once in her life, she did not know what to do.
She did not know how she would ever get off her knees and stand up again.
She did not know how she would manage to take her next breath.
She did not know how to bear the unbearable."

— Jennifer Donnelly, *The Wild Rose*

IT BEGAN IN 2018

In April 2018, on a day to celebrate my son Nicholas' graduation and soon departure to college, my father had a heart attack on his way to our house. Bob (my dad) stopped to help a stranger dislodge his car from a snowbank after a spring snowstorm pummelled the Twin Cities. Unfortunately, rather than attending our celebration, he died in the ER. Consequently, we all spent the rest of the day at the hospital. At the same time, friends cleared away the food and decorations to celebrate Nicholas' successes.

Three weeks later, as planned, we drove Nicholas 1,216 miles to his dorm and the start of his college adventure to become a chef.

Fast forward to a Saturday afternoon in September of that same year. While still grieving my dad's death, and after talking with Nicholas the evening before, a police officer came to my home to inform me that "Nicholas Seidl died unexpectedly."

That was the end of my life as I knew it and the start of another life that I never wanted.

I learned very quickly that almost no one knows or senses who to be or what to say to a mother who loses a child. I endured platitudes and advice and ignorant wisdom shared by the mouthful. I met other mothers in various stages of grief and learned from them what it is to live with a permanently broken heart. Few people are genuine, empathic, safe, understanding, or patient in the face of tragedy. I learned to isolate myself to avoid those hoping to fix me, make me feel better, or encourage me to move on. I found that people are not comfortable in the presence of a grieving mother and will do whatever it takes to escape *their* discomfort.

With Covid not far behind my tragedies and spending more time coaching than before 2018, I witnessed other coaches' reactions to tragedy and grief. I heard what they said to clients and their questions about handling the increasing stories of grief. But unfortunately, there weren't resources specific to coaches to help with these stories of sorrow and suffering. Moreover, coach training programs don't cover the skills needed in these dire circumstances.

So, regardless of the belief that coaching is not the place for challenging topics like loss, grief, and trauma, as of late, they often show up in our coaching conversations. These sorrowful clients deserve more than they commonly receive; platitudes and a referral to therapy.

Consequently, I'm here to fulfill the many coach's requests for help and our clients' hope for support. And while I don't purport comprehensive expertise, I believe there are vital and neglected skills that merit revisiting and enhancing: *conscious presence* and *witnessing*. These specific skills allow us to fulfill **who** and **what** our clients want and need during difficult and traumatic situations.

Let's get started by breaking down what these concepts mean.

SO, WHAT DOES IT MEAN TO BE CONSCIOUS?

Being *conscious* is to bring your attention to the moment's who, what, where, when, and why. Being conscious is not a talent, gift, or exclusive, nor does it become habitual—it takes deliberately focusing your attention again and again.

Consciousness is having knowledge of your existence in real-time, your surroundings, sensations, feelings, and thoughts—without interpretation, assumption, or attachment. *Consciousness* is what you might achieve when you choose to be *conscious*.

For context:

Webster's Revised Unabridged Dictionary defines **conscious** as: *Made the object of consciousness; known to oneself, possessing the faculty of knowing one's thoughts or mental operations.*

Whereas Webster's Revised Unabridged Dictionary defines **consciousness** as: *The state of being conscious; knowledge of one's own existence, condition, sensations, mental operations, acts, etc.*

In a coaching context, recognizing one's being, surroundings, thoughts, feelings, and sensations in the here and now and without attachments is to be conscious or to have consciousness. I will use both terms interchangeably from here.

CONSIDER THIS:

Taking *conscious* and *consciousness* one step further leads to asking who is doing, sensing, feeling, and thinking? Who is the one able to direct their attention and know that they exist? Who is it that might achieve *consciousness* through being decidedly *conscious*?

Awareness is knowing *who* is conscious and *who* has consciousness. Awareness knows the doer, the sensor, the feeler, and the thinker.

PAUSE AND REFLECT:

When pondering your grocery list while your client speaks, where and who are you? More importantly, where and who are you when your client tells you they are considering suicide?

WHAT DOES IT MEAN TO BE PRESENT?

Presence is the courtesy you provide your client by arriving and staying in physical, mental, and emotional attendance while participating in your coaching conversation. Consequently, most coaches appreciate that presence is a cornerstone of coaching. But imagine the impact on your client and their process when you not only attend and participate in the conversation but also *recognize yourself* as attending the conversation.

For context:

Webster's Revised Unabridged Dictionary defines **presence** as: *The state of being present or being within sight or call or at hand;— opposed to absence.*

WordNet 3.0 by Princeton University defines **presence** as: *The state of being present; current existence.*

Many coaches teach their clients the simple grounding exercise of feeling their fanny in the chair and their feet on the floor—give it a go right now if you're willing. What do you notice about yourself when you attempt presence? How might the skills of being *conscious* and *present* impact your coaching conversation? Just a hunch, but I suspect they offer the coach clarity and perhaps confidence, which may diminish feared topics a coach might knowingly or unknowingly avoid.

PAUSE AND REFLECT:

Our neocortex differentiates us from other living creatures and allows us the capacity for *consciousness* and *presence*. Yet, most of the time, we don't initiate these skills. Why do you suppose that is?

ATTENTION

Attention is the coaching agreement and your promise to focus only on your client while in a coaching session. Attention may be easier to conceptualize and attain than consciousness and presence. Yet, it can be similarly challenging to maintain.

For context:

Webster's Revised Unabridged Dictionary defines **attention** as: *An act of civility or courtesy; care for the comfort and pleasure of others.*

WordNet 3.0 by Princeton University defines **attention** as: *The faculty or power of mental concentration.*

The intersection of consciousness, presence, and attention in a coaching conversation invites richer, more dedicated participation by both participants while providing sole consideration to the client and their immediate needs. I call this convergence *conscious presence*.

PAUSE AND REFLECT:

What level of attention, presence, and consciousness does your coaching agreement include?

ACQUIRING CONSCIOUS PRESENCE

Conscious presence is a place we can reach and linger, but not a destination we'll remain. Attaining it requires persistent inner witnessing, intention, and humility, all of which we humans give ourselves much more credit for than our narcissistic and distractible minds accomplish.

WHO IS THE INNER WITNESS?

Our inner witness enables consciousness. The inner witness knows *who* senses, thinks, feels, and does and knows the motives behind the thoughts, feelings, sensations, and doing.

For context:

Webster's Revised Unabridged Dictionary defines **witness** as: *One who is cognizant; a person who beholds or otherwise has personal knowledge of anything; as an eyewitness; an earwitness. To see or know by personal presence and have direct cognizance.*

We need an inner witness to know our unabashed selves and maintain attention and *conscious presence* with our clients and their experiences. And while *witnessing* may seem like a fundamental skill for coaches, when it comes to topics that trigger fear or perhaps shame, we inevitably lose presence and our ability to witness.

For example, imagine working with a client striving to quit smoking—your chosen area of coaching and your comfort zone. But, today, they share that their son died by suicide in the last few weeks—what happens to your presence?

PAUSE AND REFLECT:

Fight, flight, freeze—what is your capacity to intentionally stay present while feeling uneasy, unstable, and potentially inadequate?

CONSIDER THIS:

We've all learned that coaching is about empowering our clients, including giving them the control to choose every session's agenda. Still, there seems to be a common perception that coaching and goals go hand-in-hand, and coaches often take the reins, galloping into goal review and goal setting. Consider again the scenario above, your client whose son died by suicide since your previous conversation. What might be the impact of asking, "How did it go this week with your goal to smoke just one cigarette a day?" Compared to, "What feels important to talk about today, Client?" Additionally, which question requires more of your conscious presence and active attention? Lastly, which question allows the client permission to choose where they want to begin?

CONSCIOUS WITNESSING

Many people seem to believe that being physically awake equates to presence. However, sitting in a chair with our eyes open merely means we're (probably) not sleeping; it doesn't mean we're present. Someone who is unconscious is an extreme example of a body's presence minus energetic, emotional, and cognitive presence.

Humans adeptly accomplish many activities with a physical presence but without energy, thought, or feeling. Two simple examples are sleeping and chemical intoxication. Then there are the daily activities we thoughtlessly undergo, such as driving a car, grocery shopping, eating, watching television, and surfing social media. By way of illustration, how often do you go looking for something and then forget what you're searching for? Or how about reading and not remembering what you've just read?

PAUSE AND REFLECT:

How might we utilize our inner witness to stay *consciously present* with our clients?

CONSIDER THIS:

The first job of our inner witness is observing our mental and emotional patterns, triggers, and habits. *Inner witnessing* happens when we see past our ego defenses to our limitations and perhaps our blind spots. When we can intentionally connect with our *inner witness*, we have the ability to *witness* another human being's suffering, just like putting our oxygen mask on first.

JOANNE

We begin with a narrative. Please read this story as though Joanne is talking to you as a client might share their story. While you read, take notice of your attention, physical sensations, emotions, and thoughts—witness your reactions.

Sunday morning

"After taking Joe (14) and Tom (13) on their paper route Sunday morning, I left the house to spend the day with my friends while the boys were with their dad at my home (a controlled environment rather than some creepy place he lived in). We were all scheduled to meet up at Joe and Tom's hockey banquet that evening, and I would bring the boys home with me afterward.

I left a thirty-minute gap between leaving home and their dad arriving—it was better if we didn't see each other face-to-face. Strangely, I passed their dad on the freeway and thought to myself, "he's early." But you kind of go, "Oh, okay," and shrug it off since the weather service predicted a heavy snowfall that day.

While at my friend's house in Maple Grove, it began snowing quite severely, so I called home to tell the kids that I was coming to the banquet and that the snow might delay my arrival. But, unfortunately, the phone was busy, busy, busy (no cell phones yet, only rotary phones). We had a phone in the upstairs bedroom, and my three Irish setters would wrestle on the bed, knocking the phone off the hook, so again, I shrugged it off. Instead, I called my neighbor and said, "would you go over and tell the kids that I'm trying to reach them and hang up the phone?"

He went over and knocked on the door, and nobody responded. He could see one of the dog crates and one of my dogs near it, but the dog didn't respond to the knock on the door. Since he had a key, he opened the door. At this point, my neighbor saw blood, heard a noise, backed out of the house, and called the cops.

I was still in Maple Grove and hadn't heard anything yet, so I called back. I got a hold of Sandy, who lived across the street from us, and she was crying. I said, "Sandy, what's wrong?" She told me, "I don't know but something's not right at your house." Then she said, "the police are coming, give me the number of where you are." So I did, and I waited.

Then I thought, "I need to leave," but I waited until the police called me. The cops asked me where I was, and I told them. Then they asked, "do you have a gun there?" I said, "I think my friend's have a gun but I'll find out." Sure enough, they did, so I told the cop. Then he said, "I want you to shut all the doors, pull all the drapes, and just stay where you are." I'm like, "what the hell?" and he said, "we're sending a sheriff to get you." So I'm thinking, "Okay...?"

So here we are, all under lockdown, and I don't know anything. My dad was an officer in the Oakdale police department part-time, and after talking with him, he drove to my house and asked to go inside. However, their response was, "nope; nobody's going in there."

At that point, two officers entered my house, saw my dead dog, and started downstairs to the basement and our family room. The officers saw part of what was down there but heard a noise in the house, and everybody pulled out.

My dad was there, on-site, and the SWAT team showed up and pretty much shot out every window on my house with tear gas. At the same time, the police took me from my friend's house to the Maple Grove police station, where we waited for the Minneapolis police to come to me.

The roads were terrible. I waited in the Maple Grove police department, not knowing anything. Finally, Minneapolis cops arrived and took me to their police station, where a Chaplain was waiting. They took me into a room and started asking me questions about the timeline of my day and what I was doing. I was asking, "what's going on here? Something bad is here; what's going on?" I told them, "you need to tell me; I need to know."

The officer looked at me and said, "your children are dead, your animals are dead, and your ex-husband is dead." What do you say to that? I went to pieces, and then the Chaplain came in. I think I was lying on the floor by that time. What can a Chaplain say at that moment? I don't know how long I was there. I finally said, "where are my children?" and the Chaplain said, "they've gone to the morgue." And I said, "what about my dogs?" and he said, "I don't know. I think maybe they went there, too."

The officer eventually said, "where do you want to go?" and I answered, "I want to go home," and he said, "you can't. You can't go there, it's not habitable." And I'm like, "Okay, I guess I have to go to my mom and dad's house in Oakdale."

It was a bad winter storm, a horrible blizzard, but they drove me out to my parents' house. I had nothing with me other than what I was wearing. From there, we all began to piece together what happened.

At one point, a police officer called to tell me, "you probably need to contact a mortuary to come and get your children's bodies." I said, "What? How? What do I tell them? Where will they go?" I wasn't thinking straight, but I finally called a mortuary. The question they asked that I wasn't expecting was, "what do you want to do with *him*?" I said I didn't care (ex-husband/father of the children). You can put him in the dumpster for all I care." They said, "We really can't do that," so I said, "well, send him along, and I'll figure that out as I figure the rest of this out."

In the meantime, I am trying to find clothes to wear and figure out how to get my money. I talked to the police, and with a shrug, they told me that I was a suspect until we had all of the reports (the coroner's report, death timeline, etcetera), and they froze my accounts.

I didn't know what had happened yet, but I knew that he (their father) had shot them. I didn't know any of the details. Later, I learned that their father used a handgun to kill Joe, Tom, and the dogs.

From what I put together, when he (their father) arrived, he went to the kitchen, where two of my dogs approached, and he immediately shot them both in the head. At that time, the boys were downstairs eating breakfast and watching TV with my other dog. Then their father went downstairs, and that's when he shot them. He came up behind Joe and shot him in the back of the head. And Tom must have gotten up and was hollering and screaming while Bo (my dog) leaped off the couch at him (ex-husband/

father), and he shot Bo in the chest. Tom lost several fingers to a bullet while trying to fight back, and then Tom was shot in the head. Then their father went upstairs and spray-painted messages on the walls, opened my closet, spray painted my clothes, and then laid down in what used to be our bedroom, which overlooked the garage. He knew I'd come in that way and waited.

My ex-husband waited for hours for me to come home; his kids and the dogs dead in the basement. But when he realized that my neighbor and the cops had discovered him, he took my shotgun and "gutshot" himself. My ex-husband did that because he didn't want to die; he would have shot himself in the head if he did. So as it turns out, he had a pretty slow death. It's not fast when you gutshot yourself, so I was grateful for that.

When the police got in there, he was dead on my bed with my gun.

So then I'm left to make all these choices. I remember praying, "I don't know what to do, and I don't know how to do it; you've got to give me some direction to walk through this." I had to make Joe and Tom's funeral arrangements. I said the boys would be in the visitation room, and *he* will be in a different part of the building. I told them, "I do not want *him* in the same room with my children." He (father/ex-husband) had a paper box casket. I told the funeral home, "I don't care what it looks like, just put him in it." So I went to his funeral and his burial. The staff wanted to give me his (armed services) flag, and I said to give it to his mother; I wanted nothing to do with it."

PAUSE AND REFLECT:

What happened to your presence and attention as you read Joanne's story?

CONSIDER THIS:

The second job of our *inner witness* is staying with our client and their story, not retreating to emotional safety. Withdrawal leads to offering platitudes like, "I can't imagine what you're going through" or "I'm sorry for your loss(es)." Our distressed clients deserve infinitely more than that. Our clients need and deserve their suffering witnessed and validated with our full attention (*conscious presence*) and empathy.

DIGGING A LITTLE DEEPER: INNER WITNESSING

What emotional and physical reactions did you notice while reading Joanne's story? Were you distressed, unsettled, or insecure? What else comes to mind? Whatever you find, look beneath it and ask yourself why?

- Did you experience heartfelt pain while embracing Joanne's suffering and sharing her burden? Why?

- Did Joanne's grief feel risky or unsafe, like an earthquake, and you noticed an urge to flee? Why?

- Perhaps you sensed yourself sinking away to the safety of your mind—you remained physically in the room but not present. What happened to you?

- Maybe something else?

SYMPATHY, PITY, AND EMPATHY

Sympathy and pity are not appropriate in any coaching conversation.

Why not sympathy or pity? The simple explanation is that they minimize and invalidate our client's experiences and remove us from the conversation.

Below is a beautifully detailed description taken from Isabel Wilkerson's courageous book, *Caste: The Origins of Our Discontents*. In it, she clarifies empathy, sympathy, and pity and then challenges us to embrace the power of *Radical Empathy*. Likewise, it's my opinion that the field of coaching would do well to adopt Ms. Wilkerson's Radical Empathy:

"Empathy is not sympathy. Sympathy is looking across at someone and feeling sorrow, often in times of loss.

Empathy is not pity. Pity looks down from above and feels a distant sadness for another person in their misfortune.

Empathy, often viewed as putting yourself in someone else's shoes and imagining how you would feel, might be a start, but that's little more than role-playing. It is not enough in our ruptured world.

*On the other hand, **radical empathy** means educating oneself and listening with a humble heart to understand another's experience from their perspective, not as we imagine we would feel. Radical empathy is not about you and what you think you would do in a situation you've never been in and perhaps never will. Instead, it is the kindred connection of deep knowing that opens your spirit to the pain of another as they perceive it."*

CONSIDER THIS:

Radically empathic coaching requires witnessing *your* emotional reactions and inner witnessing. Your emotional response to your client's experience is substantial; it demonstrates your willingness to witness and sets the stage for immediate and future relating. Your emotional response has the power to enhance or diminish your coaching relationship. There is no one appropriate and memorizable response to suffering. Consequently, *conscious presence* and inner witnessing are essential.

Let's dig into what Radical Empathy might look like in a coaching conversation.

EMBRACING THE DISCOMFORT AND DESPAIR OF GRIEF

What's your response when a client tells you a loved one has died? "I'm sorry for your loss." Or perhaps you become tongue-tied and offer, "I can't imagine what you're going through." Alternatively, your client shares that a burglary occurred with possessions destroyed and stolen at their home. What do you say to that? What if your client tells you their son is addicted to heroin? You say what?

Where do you take the conversation after tough topics like these? You might begin by thinking that these are topics for therapy, not coaching. You may want to suggest they talk to another coach because this is not your comfort zone. Still, your client is talking to you for the time being, so what do you do? Perhaps you do the safe thing and offer a socially appropriate platitude and then hope for a change in subject.

But what about the client who doesn't make it past the second interview for a new job they desperately want, an empty-nester whose youngest child has just moved out, or a client in the throes of divorce? These scenarios may not spotlight grief but involve loss, and coaches commonly hear them. So how do you support your client as they find their path forward in these situations? Hint: These experiences deserve the same care and consideration as terrifying topics like death, natural disaster, and substance abuse.

SO, WHAT'S THE PROPER RESPONSE?

Ah, if only there were a simple, generic answer. But alas, grief and trauma are topics that often rattle a coach's confidence. After assessing a topic's severity, some coaches actively change the subject! Do you offer a reflection? Ask a question? Set a goal? Which coaching skill is the next appropriate move? And, where is your attention while you contemplate what comes next?

You may wonder if it's appropriate to say, "I'm sorry?" You may ask, "what does your grief feel like?" Or maybe you invite them to look at the positive, "your loved one is in a better place now," or "things happen for a reason," or "God only gives you what you can handle." Then, maybe a semblance of the following begins forming in your mind:

I'll tell them it'll get better with time. But first, they have to take care of themselves; maybe I can offer some ideas like yoga, meditation or a grief therapist? Then, I could tell them how strong they are; after all, look at what they're going through. Finally, maybe I should ask them, "how did they die?" or "what happened?"

CONSIDER THIS:

We all experience grief during our lives, so why are we so uncomfortable with the topic? Just intuition on my part, but I suspect it's because we have an irrational hope to evade death in its entirety.

WE'RE NOT TREATING GRIEF, LOSS, OR TRAUMA

At the onset of this book, I want to clarify that *treating* grief, loss, and trauma is not the coach's objective. Treatment of any kind is for counselors and therapists and is not within the coaching scope of practice and, therefore, off-limits to coaches. What coaches can do is intentionally *witness* their clients with *conscious presence*.

LIVING WITH GRIEF: DAY 8, EULOGY

Nicholas was my "easy" child. He delighted everyone near him, including every teacher he had during his entire school career. Nicholas was the teacher's pet without fail. I remember his third-grade conference; it was "student-lead," which meant Nicholas had prepared to show me all of his achievements for the entire year. His pride showed on his smiling face and in his excited, confident voice, though he was too embarrassed to say he was proud of himself.

Nicholas had a gentle heart and cared deeply for his family. He looked after his younger brother Joey when they were small and inseparable. They chose to sleep in the same bed until they were much older than Joey would like me to say. Nicholas taught Joey how to ride a bike, build Lego creations, and do homework (that last lesson didn't stick, however). Nicholas was always patient, warm, kind, and eager to help anyone.

Nicholas liked a mental challenge, and he was headstrong. The older he became, the more Nicholas would proclaim the opposite of whatever point of view you had. However, I believe that he yearned for the security of agreement deep down.

In his early teens, Nicholas began growing, as all teen boys do, but he kept growing and growing and growing. During those years, Nicholas continually heard how handsome and tall he was, leading to an overconfident and stubborn streak. The endless compliments both increased his energy and created a fear of failure. He became so accustomed to being the golden student, worker, child, brother, and friend that he went to tragic lengths to maintain his status.

Nicholas was not a friend of moderation. (I don't know where he acquired that attribute.) Everything he did was to the nth degree. Nicholas worked hard and played hard. He explored and rested arduously. Because, of course, if you do everything to the point of exhaustion, you can escape yourself.

Nicholas was the life of the party and couldn't say no to one. If there was something fun to do, he would do it. Nicholas was so busy welcoming the entire world into his arms and carrying everyone on his shoulders that he forgot he was worthy of the same. Nicholas loved honus (Hawaiian green sea turtles), and I believe it is their tranquility and grace for which he longed.

As you told me hours before you died, Nicholas, I love you, and I miss you. I hope you have found serenity in grandpa Bob's arms, Yiyi.

IN CLOSING

Remember that support is *being with* a person experiencing a distressing emotion without trying to change, improve, or redirect anything; in other words, *witnessing*. Additionally, with conscious presence, we can witness another human being's pain without getting caught up in it. Conscious presence also supports appropriate boundaries and helps us avoid burnout. However, remember that we will do and say what's most comfortable, straightforward, and safe for ourselves without inner witnessing and conscious presence.

CLOSING INQUIRIES

I invite you to self-observe your emotional and mental reactions and challenge your inner status quo while reading this book's true accounts, scenarios, and several psychological theories. We'll utilize the Enneagram as a dynamic tool to explore **your** inner landscape and predictable stumbling blocks to *conscious presence*. If you've not heard of the Enneagram, I'll introduce you. If you're familiar with the Enneagram, I hope you uncover a helpful new perspective or two.

- What makes the topics of loss, grief, and trauma challenging for you?
- What assumptions are attached to your emotional reactions to grief, loss, and trauma?
- How might *radical empathy* impact your coaching?

"Once you can say to yourself, 'I have every right, and I will never forget,' I guess that's when you finally find some relief.
I don't expect that pain to go away anymore.
When you're anticipating the pain dissipating, it never does.
We burden ourselves with expectations of what we should or shouldn't be or do. I would imagine it's like losing a limb;
once you accept that it's not there, you can move on to the next step of getting the prosthesis. It doesn't mean you don't have phantom pain for that lost limb, but you can move forward, and you can say,
'Okay, I'll get this artificial leg, and I'll see how well I can hop around on it.' Even when it's not there,
it's always there; you know it,
and the people closest to you know it."

~ Joanne Grimsrud

CHAPTER TWO

DEFINING LOSS, TRAUMA, AND GRIEF

"Grief is a sneaky thing, always coming and going like some guest you didn't invite and can't turn away. She wants this grief, although she'd never admit it. Lately, it's the only thing that feels real."

— Kristin Hannah, *Fly Away*

In my experience, talking about loss, trauma, and grief is uncomfortable for most, causing its avoidance. But, let's face it, most of us don't take the time to explore or understand loss, trauma, and grief until it impacts us. And even then, it's not usually about understanding it but surviving it. Loss, trauma, and grief are often distressing and mysterious. Yet, how they impact our lives is crucial to supporting our clients—and even ourselves—to navigate these mucky waters. So, let's begin this chapter by defining what we mean by loss, trauma, and grief.

LOSS

Loss is a painfully familiar but sometimes unnoticed human experience. We feel it when we're transitioning—one state of being coming to an end and another beginning. Some losses are obscure. Some examples of these unrecognized losses include returning to regular work or school schedules post-vacation (or Coronavirus), moving to a new home, or completing an extensively trained sporting event (i.e., a marathon, boxing match, soccer tournament).

The intensity experienced may differ, of course, depending on the person and the circumstances. For example, an eviction or house fire probably produces more distressing emotions than inheriting and moving to a new home. Still, in all cases, something gets left behind, and something new that you may or may not want arises, which leads to feeling out of control and sometimes fear.

What happens to your emotional control when a client's story of loss triggers you? Better still, do you recognize when you're triggered?

For context:

Merriam-Webster's definition of **loss** is:

- *The act of losing possession: deprivation*
- *The harm or privation resulting from loss or separation*
- *An instance of losing*

CONSIDER THIS:

Note the word *deprivation*; it's not something we usually associate with loss, grief, or trauma. Yet, when something happens that we don't expect or want, we're deprived of control, stability, security, and perhaps safety—consider miscarriage, chronic disease, and marginalization. Deprived of attention and care, infants languish with often permanent emotional and mental consequences.

PAUSE AND REFLECT:

What are we deprived of when something we want to happen doesn't? Hope? Control? Confidence? What else?

TRAUMA

Physical or sexual assault, the unexpected or violent death of a loved one, child abuse, the death of a child, a violent accident, discrimination, or a combination of these events are but a few that lead to trauma. The emotional and mental aftermath is severe and persistent and sometimes leads to generational trauma.

Trauma emerges from a violation of our assumptions. Indeed, most of us assume that we're safe and secure in our predictable daily lives; working, eating breakfast, watching television, sleeping, etc., until the rug gets pulled out from beneath us. We go about our lives presuming we know what to expect—until life deprives us of that privilege. With our assumptions violated, safety, security, and hope evaporate; and with no guarantee that we'll get them back.

For context:

Merriam-Webster's definition of **trauma** is:

- An injury (such as a wound) to living tissue caused by an extrinsic agent
- A disordered psychic or behavioral state resulting from severe mental or emotional stress or physical injury
- An emotional upset

For our purposes, let's focus on the second definition. What does a *disordered psychic or behavioral state* mean, and how does it apply here?

Assuming most people reading this book have heard of dissociative identity disorder (DID), previously known as Multiple Personality Disorder, we know that trauma such as extreme childhood abuse elicits a psychological self-preservation response. In this case, an example of a *disordered psychic state* is creating distinct personalities who take on separate roles to protect the abused child emotionally.

Another example might be a *disordered psychic state* of anxiety or depression (or both) following a traumatic loss—the traumatic grief that follows might lead some people to a *disordered behavioral state* of substance use or abuse as a means of self-medicating.

PAUSE AND REFLECT:

What comes up for you when you consider these definitions of trauma? What other examples of *disordered psychic or behavioral state can you think of?*

WHAT'S THE COACH'S ROLE IN TRAUMATIC EVENTS?

Sometimes, people who experience trauma find it difficult or nearly impossible to talk about their experience, leading to secrecy and shame. However, the long-term effect of internalized trauma can have physical, emotional, and mental consequences. In his book, *Finding Meaning: The Sixth Stage of Grief,* David Kessler discusses that over time hidden trauma can cause depression and illnesses like cancer and heart disease, emotional instability, and alarmingly higher death rates.

In contrast, Tedeschi, Shakespeare-Finch, Taku, and Calhoun's book, *Posttraumatic Growth, Theory, Research, and Applications*, demonstrate that disclosing traumatic experiences with a safe person or writing them down, their physical, emotional, and mental manifestations of trauma improve.

Narratives allow protected processing of painful experiences and, over time, the ability to weave the event into a new reality. In addition, frequent sharing of the traumatic account invites self-reflection, stimulating emotional and mental development rather than imprisonment.

With the expansion of insight and possibility, minds and hearts open to hope, improving depression, anxiety, blood pressure, and the immune system while decreasing stress hormones like cortisol and adrenaline. Consequently, a trusted person(s) listening intently to a traumatic narrative is an integral component of healing trauma.

CONSIDER THIS:

I met a young mother whose sister regularly babysat her eighteen-month-old son while she worked. One day, her son fell down a flight of stairs while at her sister's home, and he died shortly after the fall. Two years later, the young mother, understandably bereft, had never asked her sister what happened that day—how her son came to fall down the stairs to his death.

This young mom was afraid of alienating herself from her family. She wondered if his fall wasn't accidental because she couldn't picture the event as described by her brother-in-law, yet she would not challenge the story with her sister.

Aside from an inconsistent grief group, this young mother wouldn't allow herself to grieve because she feared burdening those around her; family, friends, and coworkers. She didn't take time off of work to grieve; instead, she went to work and pretended no tragedy had befallen her.

She was shy, confused, and ashamed of her grief when I met her. She blamed herself for working rather than being with her son that day. She couldn't seem to move on from the day he died and lived in the shadows for fear of offending anyone and everyone. She was depressed and physically shrunken, yet the grieving mother oozed emotion with just a gentle inquiry about memories of her son.

Sadly, inadequate support, empathy, and love prevented this young mother from integrating her tragic loss into her present life, giving her little hope for a future.

CONSIDER THIS:

In contrast, another mother lost her son tragically to the opioid epidemic currently ravaging our country. Rather than being eighteen months old, he was eighteen years old. This mom didn't know her son was using drugs until she gathered his belongings from his dorm room and some of his friends came to pay respects.

Unlike the mother above, this mom asked friends and school staff to learn what happened despite the shock of losing her son. Then, while going through the required legal motions, she asked people for answers. She sought grief therapy and support groups within days of her son's death and had people nearby to help with household tasks and daily necessities.

This mom took some time away from work, though not long, but didn't try to hide her grief as she reentered working, and even there, people were patient and paused when emotions proved too immense to contain. At work, the people around her listened to her stories with compassion and empathy, often offering a kind touch or a hug.

All this support isn't to say that this mom wasn't suffering; indeed, she was. However, she felt free to talk about her son and retell her story whenever she needed. Additionally, though her son's death was considered a horrific accident like the previous mother's, this mom followed up with key people to learn what happened and pursue legal options.

CONSIDER THIS:

This story does not demonstrate that mom number two eliminated suffering from her life and moved on with a bright future while the first mother did not. Instead, it points to the potential long-term effects of having emotional support and trusted people who will patiently listen as grief takes refuge in a person's entirety. In addition, mom number two knew she didn't have to survive on her own, while mom number one went through everything by herself.

PAUSE AND REFLECT:

Imagine the impact of losing a child with no support at all; how would your future look?

GRIEF

IN REAL LIFE

Grief is emotional suffering, sometimes called sorrow, resulting from loss and trauma. Grief becomes a part of our life's tapestry as it is an ongoing process that ebbs and flows. While some losses and traumas are swift and complete (a massive heart attack), others last years (chronic disease and discrimination, for instance), the ensuing emotional torment of grief has no end. Grief is an endurance activity that not only deserves recognition but demands it.

For example, grief shows up in unexpected places, such as when we shelter in place during a pandemic. Unable to share our holidays, graduations, and funerals with loved ones, we suffer the loss of our freedom, routine, family and friends, and maybe our lifestyle. We grieve companionship, love, and celebration during quarantine. Grief may suffuse our homes when we've lost our traditions and way of life. And as we've seen with the demand and burnout of coaches, counselors, and therapists, grief is everywhere.

Another obscure example is sorting and purging dozens of boxes filled with years worth of our children's schoolwork. Spending time musing our children's younger years; keeping our favorite pieces while saying goodbye to others, we experience loss. It can be heart-wrenching choosing items for the 'to go' pile, staying objective and intentional, knowing we can't keep everything. For a moment, we grieve each time we say goodbye to the twenty-fourth piece of colored paper with glued fall leaves now littering the entire box of memorabilia. We're enclosed in a grief bubble while reminiscing and discarding cherished keepsakes.

More problematic for coaches are stories of a client bearing the despair of suicide, overdose, or the murder of a loved one. This client's entire dwelling is dark, contaminated, and suffocating. These grievers find no open windows or doors in which to leave, trapped within a nightmare for the foreseeable future. They are subject to a barrage of intrusive thoughts, memories, and feelings day and night. These despondent people might have lost their sense of purpose and meaning in life.

For context:

Dictionary.com defines **grief** as a *keen mental suffering or distress over affliction or loss; sharp sorrow; painful regret. A cause or occasion of keen distress or sorrow.*

Take note here that grief comprises our cognitive and emotional systems. *Keen mental suffering* is easy enough to identify as a product of the mind, but what does it mean? How does one *suffer mentally*? I suggest that anxiety is the mind's approach to suffering—thoughts that travel on an endless loop, causing unending worry and fear.

Distress and *sorrow* are emotional reactions to losing something valued, such as a person or our control. For example, when we're small children, we feel *distressed* when separated from caregivers. Additionally, *distress* is sometimes a precursor to panic, a more active version of *distress*. For example, panic might rouse us to resolve *distress* if its cause continues unattended.

PAUSE AND REFLECT:

What power does grief hold as you contemplate its meaning in your life? How might grief's impact on you interfere with your ability to coach?

THE PROMISE OF GRIEF

I will find you.

It's safe to say that grief will impact all of us during our lifetime and eventually affect others when we die. But unfortunately, there is often no completion or closure with trauma or grief. Only with time do we learn to assimilate the addition of its suffering to our emotional home; it is an unwelcome extension fraught with painful memories, emotions, and thoughts.

Concerning a loved one's death, at first, it feels as though our entire emotional residence is saturated with despair, with nowhere to escape its talons. Whether awake or asleep, we involuntarily ruminate about our loved one's life and death. We speculate what was, what should be, and what will never be. We fear losing our connection to our loved one if we don't always keep them in mind. We worry others will forget them if their memory doesn't permeate every emotional chamber of our existence.

Over time, the quantity of emotional chambers brimming with suffering reduces while windows and doors begin to open. Sometimes, however, a desolate heart overtakes the emerging emotional boundaries, and we flounder amidst grief's totality again. Yet, remarkably, we don't want the anguish to end; while there's pain, our loved one is real, we feel connected to them, and our love counts for something.

We're told we must go on living which includes accepting they're gone, and that's just too final. We've become fully subject to grief's torment and will wearily claw our way out only when we can drop no further into its sorrowful cavity.

As more time passes, there might be just one sorrowful room left sheltering despair within our emotional residence. Then, finally, an objective dynamic entry and exit appear, and we learn to develop a tolerable relationship with its mournful contents. Sometimes, we have the courage and the need to spend time with our suffering, redecorating and rearranging the furniture, and being with our sorrow. This new, unwelcome, yet permanent emotional addition has changed the entire residence's structure and design, yet wandering the halls and stepping in by choice brings fresh perspectives and, one day, perhaps wisdom instead of torment.

Only then may we understand that love does not cease with physical death.

TRYING TO DODGE GRIEF

In my experience, humans avoid grief at all costs despite knowing we'll experience it during our lives. Consequently, we seem to sense its sharp-edged cruelty and make choices in hopes of keeping it at bay.

For example, most of us have stayed in relationships because 'it's better than being alone.' Or maybe we jump from one relationship to another in hopes of outmaneuvering the void left by a missing partner. Perhaps we stayed in a job we disliked because it was better than a job unknown. Sadly, many of us are guilty of keeping an ill pet alive to postpone the pain *we* would endure with their passing. As for our human companions and family members, how many medical treatments must they bear to delay our pain? And what of ourselves; how far will we go to avoid losing our time on earth?

Our talent for averting loss occurs in coaching conversations, too. The coaching relationship offers a secure space for uncomfortable conversations, but who creates the safety, and what does security look like in a conversation? Unfortunately, diverting an emotionally challenging topic in coaching conversations is common and akin to a bait and switch—"Please bring anything to our conversations, Client, except for what makes me uncomfortable."

Imagine your client asks, "Will I be alone forever if they break up with me?" You, the coach, might say, "What if you are?" or "Don't be silly." But what about the discomfort that arises when your client shares something particularly dreadful? For example, when your client discloses that their daughter died of an overdose over the weekend. Chances are, you'll instinctively circumvent your discomfort by unconsciously locating a swift exit point. This parent's loss is complex and nightmarish; many coaches would likely search for a more comfortable and stable topic, perhaps asking how they're taking care of themselves rather than asking about their client's emotional experience.

CONSIDER THIS:

Our training to abandon topics that cause discomfort begins when we're young; after all, we witness adults invalidating and redirecting difficult conversations when we're small children. For instance, as a child, perhaps you wanted to save an injured baby bird, and the adults in your life said the baby bird would die without its mother, so there was nothing to be done, simultaneously breaking your heart. Or perhaps you wanted to save a mouse scurrying around your bedroom, and your parents firmly stated that they're destructive and dirty and should be destroyed, not coddled.

In both examples, your innocence and compassion met a practical adult mind, diminishing your hope to care for something smaller than you. We learn to evaluate what deserves care and what doesn't from the adults in our life—what merits our kindhearted attention and what does not.

PAUSE AND REFLECT:

Avoiding uncomfortable topics may be modeled and taught, but that doesn't mean it's humane or compassionate. We (adults and coaches) can learn to be with uncertainty and discomfort with intention and practice. We can create a safe and inviting space for our distressed and grieving clients and model courage while facing fear, the unknown, and despair.

A LIFETIME OF LOSSES

So far, we've covered several ways loss, trauma, and grief show up in our lives, those we notice and label, and those we feel but give no name. Below, we'll explore several chronologically typical losses and other scenarios often included in our human existence but perhaps noticed less directly than death. For ease, each topic has a relevant heading.

TODDLERHOOD

Experiencing loss begins when our parents start setting boundaries, telling us 'no.' And as all parents know, the aftermath of a child hearing 'no' can be dreadful! We humans simply don't like being deprived of something we have or want.

PAUSE AND REFLECT:

Imagine when you were young and didn't get the super sweet, marshmallowy cereal you wanted—can you remember your reaction?

PRIMARY AND SECONDARY SCHOOL YEARS

We move from elementary school to middle school and then to high school—with each transition starting over just when it feels like we've got our footing—we lose what's familiar and begin afresh, only to do it again in a few years.

PAUSE AND REFLECT:

How about the first time a boyfriend or girlfriend broke up with you—how did you feel?

At the end of the secondary educational chapter of our lives, maybe we graduated high school or received our GED and moved away to college, losing our friends, security, family, and routine. Our early life seems to be a continual ebbing and flowing of calm and turbulent waters to navigate.

MARRIAGE

Even something as seemingly joyful as a wedding bears grief. For those who choose to marry and have a traditional public wedding, the planning and preparation can be intense, often for months or years. And then, it's over in what feels like an instant. The day speeds by so quickly that it's hard to remember all the details. Then, when it is over and we settle into a new life, the vacancy of excitement can mirror a balloon deflating, slowly and noisily, until it's void of air.

HAVING CHILDREN

Next in our conventional timeline might be having our first child. Mom stays busy and focused on preparation with physical changes, a hundred books to read, a room to decorate, a hospital bag to pack, doctor appointments, and ultrasounds. And don't forget the baby showers and parties to celebrate the pregnancy and growing baby.

Then, the anticipation is over, and the baby arrives! There's a transition to a new role and a sense of purpose for parents, though it may not be as easy as reported. Everyone is excited about this new family member yet misses sleep and freedom. Likewise, mom's hormone party and sleep deprivation unleash a frequent loss of sanity.

PARENTHOOD/MOTHERHOOD

A mother might notice a loss when she stops breastfeeding—she may struggle with her sense of purpose at this significant transition period with precious bonding time lost. A similar feeling may erupt when the youngest child heads to kindergarten.

With each step children take toward independence, boundaries surface, and the emotional bonds widen. Infertility can shatter hope and meaning—realizing one won't experience an essential human capacity leaves a deep and festering wound.

RETIREMENT AND EMPTY-NESTING

Retirement and empty-nesting frequently carry a loss of routine and a sense of purpose. Commonly, our identity gets wrapped up in our occupation, and when we permanently leave our vocation, we might sense a loss of ourselves. Regrettably, people become attached to professional and parental titles, which can cause us to stumble without them.

Likewise, when the last of our children leave home, the physical loss can induce a lost sense of purpose. It makes no difference whether we're looking forward to the kids being out of the house and our retirement; it can feel like giving up something for nothing. Of course, in reality, we never stop being a parent or having skills that go beyond what's earned us a paycheck, but it doesn't feel that way when we're in the thick of loss.

AGING

As we age, we cling to what and who we once were. Focusing on our losses, we relinquish the present moment. Instead, we focus on how fast we were at our sport, how much we weighed, our injury-free body, our smooth and unblemished skin, how much hair we had, energy, health, a reliable memory, and confidence. We enthusiastically fight age with surgery, elixirs, poisons, waxes, hair color, transplants, and implants. The list of avoidance tactics goes on and on. The deprivation of and desperation for youth is glaringly poignant in humans.

PANDEMIC

Collectively, Covid-19 ravaged assumptions, liberty, and security. As a result, we lost our way of life and freedom. Over time, we lost hope and struggled to find meaning. We lost leadership, collaboration, and safety. We grieved connection, activities, and traditions. We postponed weddings and rituals that honor death. We deferred doctor visits, received delayed diagnoses, and died from untreated illnesses. We felt trapped in our own homes, some experiencing abuse and even death with no outlet for anxiety.

Our status, image, and reputation became irrelevant with few social and sporting opportunities. And of course, there are thousands of lives lost worldwide from this virus; likewise, for those in healthcare who experience a sense of purpose and identity in what they do, feeling ineffectual against this new virus and losing countless patients, some lives ended by their own hands.

We endured perpetual individual and collective losses without an end in sight while watching the world change via news channels, documentaries, and social media.

ADDICTION AND MENTAL ILLNESS

Grief may be a daily experience as we watch our loved ones struggle or suffer from addiction or mental illness. Addiction and mental illness deprive the afflicted person of choice and their loved ones of certainty while supplying both with fear and despair. As a result, their lives may become an unpredictable emotional battleground for the diagnosed and their family. Additionally, a secondary loss may arise as family members contemplate a future their loved one is entitled to but may never have. And if treatment fails (medical or psychological), there's endless anxiety in knowing their loved one's life is in danger.

PHYSICAL ILLNESS OR DISEASE

Terminal illness, chronic disease, and a permanent physical or mental disability induce torment and loss to patients and loved ones. They'll all grieve the past and an unrealized, indefinitely changed future, resulting in secondary grief. Where once the ground felt steady, uncertainty and insecurity contest core beliefs and assumptions.

TRAUMATIC DEATH

Child death or disappearance, suicide, drug overdose, and unexpected death are where true hopelessness and despair lay; amongst anger, disbelief, unreality, panic, turmoil, confusion, and sorrow. With fundamental core beliefs obliterated, there is no meaning or purpose.

Sudden death and spousal death elicit grief that is similar to child loss. We lose our footing and falter significantly. Our bedrock and fundamental convictions erode, and we grieve our previous dependability and security. We become sparse as we imagine life without our loved ones and mourn our future and past.

ABDUCTION

We hear of child abduction but never think it could happen to us. The grievers experience no closure without knowing what happened to their child or loved one. Instead, memories and imagination torment their days and nights with what-ifs and what could have been. The unknown leads to distress comparable to the families living with a loved one's suicide or drug overdose—there are too many horrific unanswered questions.

MARGINALIZATION, DISCRIMINATION, AND INTERSECTIONALITY

Marginalization, discrimination, racism, and intersectionality deprive people of their fundamental human rights and can lead to several classes of generational trauma. Disadvantages due to social, monetary, or familial circumstances and based on the judgment of others are brutal and scarring. Safety, security, and innocence end up abandoned when one's childhood is dangerous, self-perpetuating, and offers little chance of escape.

Additionally, judgment based on gender, sexual orientation, socioeconomic or social status, job title, and any other characteristic consciously or unconsciously identified and used to evaluate someone's inherent value or worth creates separation and possibly isolation, resulting in a loss of relatedness, at a minimum.

Furthermore, a person's marginalized status impacts their right to emotional validity. In particular, grief associated with loss and trauma often receives more validation, attention, and compassion when the griever is white. Further, white people seem licensed to tell their stories, expecting others to listen. For that reason, they are more likely to seek out and receive professional emotional support than their non-white counterparts.

Tragically, non-whites and marginalized populations often anticipate emotional negation of their suffering. Further, they often don't expect to receive their white counterparts' empathy and compassion, and cultural stigma may influence distrust and aversion to sharing emotional hardships. Thus, non-whites and marginalized populations are less likely to talk about their grief, loss, and trauma. And as you recall, vital to the assimilation of grief and trauma is telling our stories to trusted, caring individuals.

CONSIDER THIS:

First, imagine how you might feel and react to a white client telling you of their child's murder. Then, consider your reaction to a person of color saying the same.

PAUSE AND REFLECT:

What did you notice? Be honest with yourself.

CONSIDER THIS:

Imagine a white coach who is also a mother whose son died of a drug overdose when he was eighteen years old. Then, imagine this coach's client, a black mother whose son died at eighteen years old while selling drugs.

PAUSE AND REFLECT:

What potential biases, projections, and implications does this coaching relationship face without the coach's conscious presence and radical empathy? What potential connection might these women make with the coach's conscious presence and radical empathy?

CONSIDER THIS:

Imagine the suicide of an affluent white suburban husband and father and the outcry of support his family might receive. How might that differ for the family of an urban married transgender parent's suicide?

PAUSE AND REFLECT:

Do you recognize the compounded losses in the above three examples? Not only are individuals and families impacted by traumatic grief, but assumptions and judgments tied to the victim's identities could tragically rob the survivors of empathy, relatedness, and humanity.

Recall the two mothers mentioned earlier in this chapter who tragically lost their sons. One mother had almost no resources available to support her loss and, at that time, seemed unable to move forward from the day her eighteen-month-old son died. In contrast, mom number two had a life surrounded by people who cared and were there to catch her if she fell.

To illustrate marginalization's impact on the experience of grief, mom number one is Hmong, and mom number two is white. The shame holding hostage the young Hmong mother's entire being, including her belief that her needs don't matter, that her grief didn't matter, was unmistakable. Her young son tragically died, and she had no one with whom to share her burden except an infrequent, low attendance grief group for grieving parents.

PAUSE AND REFLECT:

Topics like murder or violent death are not only for news sensationalism; they are anyone's experience and will arise in our coaching conversations.

Can you admit to the potential impact of marginalization, racism, and discrimination on requesting or receiving deserved emotional support? What are you willing to do to change this grossly damaging endemic pattern?

THE COACH

So, how do you hold your emotional reactions (stress response) in check and stay *consciously present* with your client's experience when the topic is impossibly loaded? How do you stay *centered* with a multitude of free-flowing grief categories?

First, you are already starting this journey and heading in a compassionate direction by reading this book. I'm throwing the examples in this chapter at you because they happen. You can hope that you'll never encounter a story as horrific as those we've explored so far, yet if you are a coach for long enough and talk to enough people, you will confront similar stories. The bottom line: all of the people in your care need you to stay *consciously present* with them and *witness* their suffering.

Okay, you're present and witnessing, but you'd like to know what's safe to say. For now, don't worry about what to say; it's enough to remember the value of staying present in the space that you and your client create and provide them with your *conscious* attention.

Lastly, I'd like to mention that when grief maintains its grip with no signs of improvement for a year, it's likely not what's considered 'normal' grief. Normal grief ebbs and flows, though unpredictably, yet over time, it begins to lessen, and the griever can start assimilating their feelings. However, when grief maintains its momentum, not giving reprieve from sorrow and despair, it's considered 'complicated' grief or 'persistent complex bereavement disorder' at about the year mark.

I share this so you have a grief timeline benchmark. If you're working with a client whose grief seems emotionally unchanged after a year, it's time to refer to counseling or therapy if you haven't done so already.

LIVING WITH GRIEF: DAY 25, I AM FRACTURED

Twenty-five days into my new life.

Hollow. Fractured. Despair. Rage. Misunderstood. Exhausted. These words describe the entirety of my feelings. That's it. Sometimes I criticize myself because I feel "overly dramatic." Then I remember the police officer in my home saying, "the Dutchess County police department in New York contacted us and said Nicholas Seidl died unexpectedly." Or something of that ilk. All I accurately remember is "Nicholas died unexpectedly." Over and over and over. My child died unexpectedly. No do-overs. No second chances. Done. Final.

What do I do next? What do I do? I want to tell the officer to take it back. I want to wake up. It just cannot be true.

But now it's day twenty-five, and the truth has not changed. After gathering Nicholas' things from his dorm room, visiting the New York state police, and a funeral home, I have a permanent vision of my dead son's face to remind me of the unchangeable truth.

Nicholas was loved by so many. How can it be that we will never see his smile again? How can it be that he died alone at age eighteen?

One of his many dear friends spent time with me today, telling me stories of his antics at work. He loved working at Brasa, and it showed. Claire said to me, "He was always smiling at work and it made everyone's day to work with him! That happiness was a constant. If you knew you were working with him, it was gonna be a good and energetic shift."

He was my large child, and his departure has left a large hole in my heart where his presence used to be. I am fractured and don't know how the pieces fit together anymore.

IN CLOSING

Imagine the function of a life buoy in the water; the modest but sturdy ring physically embraces and supports a sinking and exhausted person so that they can safely rest and catch their breath. The life buoy doesn't eliminate the surrounding water, nor will it remove the person from the water; it is a benevolent guardian that provides space, safety, and hope at just the right moment.

You get to be the life buoy for your clients. While naming feelings brings objectivity to experience, it's vital to recognize that for folks experiencing trauma and substantial grief, the goal is not to help them gain objectivity by ushering them into naming their feelings—their wounds may be too deep and perhaps too fresh to start with that. Instead, these folks are drowning in powerful emotions and struggling to stay afloat; they need a life buoy to withstand intense waves of emotion without suppression or inflation.

CLOSING INQUIRIES

Our objective as coaches is not to assuage or remove painful feelings such as grief and sorrow; it's to be *consciously present* with our clients no matter who they are, their circumstances, or their emotions. We are responsible for recognizing *our* reactions and setting ourselves aside to maintain objectivity and *witness* our clients. In this way, we are providing safety, hope, and purpose.

- What, if anything, surprises you about the definitions of grief, loss, and trauma?

- What's an example of loss in your life that you didn't recognize as such until now?

- What biases do you hold that might impact your coaching equality?

"Be very careful to take the lead from [your] client and not to impose labels, reflections, or the potential for Posttraumatic Growth if that is not evident in the language the client is using."

— Richard G Tedeschi, Jane Shakespeare-Finch, Kanako Taku, Lawrence G. Calhoun, *Posttraumatic Growth, Theory, Research, and Applications*

CHAPTER THREE

THINKING ABOUT THE MIND

"If we whites want to interrupt this system, we have to get racially uncomfortable and be willing to examine the effects of our racial engagement. This includes not indulging in whatever reactions we have—anger, defensiveness, self-pity, and so forth—in a given cross-racial encounter without first reflecting on what is driving our reactions and how they will affect other people."

– Robin DiAngelo, *White Fragility*

THE MIND

Our mind provides us with memory, feelings, and temperament, among other things. These qualities merge with our human experiences to deliver a socially sound, responsive, and operable emotional system. This commingling of neurobiology and nurture produces the personality we use to greet the people, places, and things in our lives.

The question is, are you *consciously present* with what life brings each day?

CONSIDER THIS:

Pretend you're beginning your day at the computer. Rather than mechanically walking through your day, today, you take the time to *witness* your thoughts and feelings. Perhaps you notice the following emotional reactions to your morning tasks:

1. *Overwhelm* as you see your email inbox.

2. *Relief* as you make your way through the emails.

3. Perhaps momentary *frustration* or *relief* as you turn away from your lengthy inbox to take a phone call.

4. Later, maybe *competence* as you support your client's journey.

5. How about *excitement* hearing about a client's achievements.

6. And perhaps *dismay* when your client discloses receiving a multiple sclerosis diagnosis.

7. You might feel *discomfort* as you ask for a payment.

8. And *gratitude* for your client's preparedness with a check in hand.

9. Then there's *irritation* while seeking compensation from an insurance company.

10. And *appreciation* for the person at the insurance company that resolves the issue for you.

PAUSE AND REFLECT:

Why is it beneficial to identify our emotional reactions? First, because coaches know the benefit of naming their emotions. Second, coaches need to 'walk the talk' for the ability to mirror their clients. Third, coaches need to recognize their mind's innate reactions at the onset of a familiar emotion. And finally, coaches are responsible for avoiding patterned emotional reactions in a client's presence.

NEURAL PATHWAYS

Our mind's interpretation of emotions and subsequent responses takes only a split second. Once the neocortex identifies an emotion, it slides straight down its familiar neural pathway, and we react as we always do. So how might your unchecked automatic emotional reaction after hearing a client's story impact your conversation?

To demonstrate how quick this emotion/reaction exchange happens, pretend you received a "not at this time, but thank you" email after the third interview for an exciting new job; how might you feel? Disappointed, rejected, embarrassed, shame, hopeless, surrender? These feelings are easily accessed because you've felt them before—your mind knows where to locate them quickly. Think about how often you've felt disappointed in your lifetime. Probably many because disappointment often accompanies the word 'no.'

Over the years, repetition gives rise to a 'disappointment' cache in our mind, which innately activates with comparable experiences; feeling disappointed when you couldn't have the action figure belonging to your childhood friend. Or today, when your client tells you they are switching coaches. Ouch.

Predictability is our mind's gatekeeper; it scans and hones in on experiences that reinforce memories, knowledge, feelings, and even actions. Our mind seeks to pair our recent and past experiences, much like fingerprint matching. You have a new experience, and without awareness, a corresponding emotional cache opens, providing a habitual response, thus, reinforcing its neural pathway. It's easy to see that over years of repetition, we're not likely to react in any way other than what we've rehearsed countless times—unless we're aware of our habitual responses in real-time. Only then can we work at cultivating a different response and outcome, thus creating a new neural pathway.

Our emotional reactions may not always be substantial. By that, I mean not everyone has an urge to cry when something is sad or yell when angry. Likewise, consistent with the triggered emotion's narrative, present conditions, and unique history, we may sometimes under-react or respond incongruently to a presenting challenge.

For example, I began wearing glasses when I was two years old and went through elementary school with the unsurprising nickname, 'four-eyes.' Contact lenses were available to me when I was fourteen years old. In just one afternoon, my life changed. In the summer between eighth and ninth grade, I went from unknown and unpopular to well-known and appealing. All because my corrective eyewear came out of a frame and onto my eyes! Consequently, to this day, I dislike wearing glasses in public. In this way, I've acquired an exaggerated sense of shame at the mere idea of people seeing me in glasses—I am overreacting (thanks to my inner critic) because of an ancient shame cache and eyewear neural pathway.

A flip-side example might be someone having divorced parents as a teenager and feeling accustomed to the two-household routine. Then a friend laments and sobs because her parents are divorcing. Feelings related to the end of your friend's in-tact family are new to her; she's drowning in unfamiliar emotions. Without affect or empathy, maybe you tell her, "It's going to be fine; you'll get used to it." In this scenario, your response may feel unsupportive and disinterested to your heartbroken friend—a reaction that falls short of the support she wants. Your familiarity (neural pathway) with divorced parents caused you to under-react to your friend's experience.

Distraction (lacking presence) might also cause under-reaction. Again, using the previous example of divorcing parents, let's say your mind is on a recent fight with your partner. This time, you reply to your friend's plight with a nod and quiet grunt, leaving her to experience you as insensitive and distant.

SELF-AWARENESS

Do you notice or pay attention to your emotional reactions when having a conversation? Perhaps you smile or laugh when feeling joy? When you're curious, maybe you scrunch your forehead and lean in. When surprised, do your eyebrows lift, or does your breathing change? When afraid, you might breathe shallowly and physically retreat, or maybe you talk fast. When you're angry, do you clench your teeth while your heart races? What do you feel when you're at a loss for words with a client?

A coach's self-regulation is essential so that our conversations remain focused on our clients, not on protecting ourselves from a painful, uncomfortable, or shocking topic. Coaches must recognize their triggers and subsequent reactions to do their best coaching.

CONSIDER THIS:

Despite a primarily self-absorbed demeanor, introspection seems troublesome for most humans. Indeed, we often demonstrate our egocentric human nature by claiming personal insight. However, objective self-observation is not innate or organic; it requires consistent practice and eternal humility. Undoubtedly, genuine self-awareness annuls any claim of insight, wisdom, calling oneself an 'empath,' or any other attribute that we hope will provide us coaching credibility and admiration. (In other words, by claiming humility, we nullify humility.)

PAUSE AND REFLECT:

How do we practice *inner witnessing* when we realize declaring it doesn't make it so? Enter a meditation or presence practice.

MEDITATION OR PRESENCE PRACTICE

First, let's address any assumptions and eye rolls by naming what we think or believe meditation to be and what benefits we think it might offer. For a start, I've heard meditation described with the following range of words:

Calming, a quiet mind, an empty mind, not thinking, knowing oneself, spirituality, deep breathing, mantra, a buzzword, Eastern religion, Buddha, monks, contemplative practice, enlightenment, yoga, boring, useless, impossible, hard to do, non-productive, what else?

For context:

Webster's Revised Unabridged Dictionary defines **meditation** as:

- *The act of meditating; close or continued thought; the turning or revolving of a subject in one's mind; serious contemplation; reflection; musing.*

- *Thought; without regard to kind.*

The *reflection* or *musing* mentioned above is often the practice of noticing the breath as we inhale and exhale. Alternatively, we might have a mantra, chant, or prayer as a *serious contemplation*. But note that there's no indication of one way, place, time, or duration to meditate.

What's the point, goal, or intention of meditation? The outcome for one who regularly practices meditation, breathing, presence, or prayer is much like the athlete who practices their sport—practice to develop the neural pathways and stamina for select activation—the product of practiced meditation is ***conscious presence.***

CONSIDER THIS:

Meditation includes noticing but not holding onto our thoughts. However, emotions may arise if we get carried away with a notion, making it harder to detach from said thought. Can you trust that whatever thought and feeling drifting through your attention will be there when your practice is complete?

PAUSE AND REFLECT:

What's your definition and experience of meditation?

CONSCIOUS PRESENCE

So, how does a meditation practice help when encountering complex thoughts and emotions and the patterned responses our neural pathways provide? When our mind (unconsciously) recognizes an uncomfortable or undesirable feeling, patterned neural pathways activate, and we go offline, even with clients. Therefore, *conscious presence*, the byproduct of regular meditation, is the only genuine method for staying objectively present with an emotionally charged topic.

Meditation is more than carving out time in your day to sit still and clear your mind. Meditation—**presence**—is for sharing, not isolating. In other words, we should invite the *conscious presence* we gain from our solo meditation practice into the rest of our lives; brushing our teeth, talking to a friend, exercising, coaching, etc. So, while scheduling a time to meditate daily is vital, the intangible changes obtained from meditation impact our functional daily lives. By way of example, along with strength, weight-lifting has the added practical benefit of easing activities like lifting a heavy bag of garbage, gardening, and bathing your dog in the bathtub.

CONSIDER THIS:

We can conjure presence with a consistent meditation practice at any time; washing the dishes, brushing our teeth, and walking our clean dog. When we engage in a daily presence practice, its calming impact shows up when faced with everyday challenges. Much like salivating when we think of a favorite meal, *conscious presence* can arrive with a practiced cue.

PAUSE AND REFLECT:

How might *conscious presence* affect taking a walk in nature?

What do we gain with grounding and *conscious presence*? The ability to call ourselves back from an emotional disappearing act. Meditation is a long-term strategy for presence, recognizing our distractability, and getting us back in the conversation.

INNER WITNESSING IS UNIQUE TO HUMANS

Witnessing our thoughts, feelings, and actions is unique to humans and goes by a few names, such as (but not limited to): self-awareness, self-reflection, inner observation, inner witnessing, and insight. Helen Palmer, one of the co-founders of the Narrative Enneagram, calls this capacity our Inner Observer. Because we have this unique ability, I believe we have an essential responsibility to use it for our personal development and others' good. So the question is; how do we find and learn to use our ability to self-witness?

First, you have to meet your inner witness. It is always running in the background: like breathing, it is self-regulating. Still, we don't often consciously engage with its wisdom, maybe because we don't yet know how to do so? Connecting with your inner witness is how mindfulness, meditation, grounding, and *conscious presence* enter the picture.

YOUR INNER WITNESS

You might think of your inner witness as your conscience, but it's not quite the same. Your inner witness observes your thoughts, feelings, and actions without judgment, evaluation, or agenda. In contrast, your conscience evaluates and steers your choices to avoid feeling bad—your conscience has an objective to feel good about your decisions.

Think about a time when you did something to trigger your conscience— maybe you took a library book without checking it out properly, wore your sister's sweater without asking, or perhaps you cheated to get a new account at work. How did you feel, and what was your response when you noticed your conscience waving a flag to get your attention? Perhaps you put back the library book, admitted your trespass to your sister, and fessed up to your misdeed at work. Or maybe, to diminish the guilty feelings your conscience warned against, you justified your falsehoods as not hurting anyone, payback, or perhaps deserving or entitled.

Connecting with our inner witness is a bit like hide-and-seek—you'll more quickly find the hider if you're quiet and listen rather than running all over willy-nilly looking behind every curtain and under every bed. Your *inner witness* is probably hiding in plain sight if you slow down long enough to see with more than just your eyes; you need to listen and sense.

BLIND SPOTS

By way of values and emotions, your conscience lets you know when you've stepped outside the limits (I feel bad about ...). By contrast, your inner witness has no agenda and will not encourage or discourage you in any direction. Instead, your inner witness is an unbiased mirror that sees the real you rather than who you internalize and project to the world. Consequently, your inner witness knows your tricks and protective measures, known as blind spots and shadows. Examples of blind spots and shadows might be withdrawal, manipulation, passive aggression, judgment, and bullying, to name a few.

Blind spots are not feelings of guilt or shame that your conscience accentuates when you make a crummy choice but the actions that may or may not trigger your conscience. Your inner witness can reveal blind spots to offer you options and awareness of feelings, actions, and reactions.

CONSIDER THIS:

A few examples using the three scenarios above:

1. Why did you take the library book? Perhaps you forgot your library card and didn't want to go home to get it. Possible blind spot:

   - Thinking you're above the rules—perhaps telling yourself, "Just this once won't hurt anything."

2. Why didn't you ask your sister for permission to wear her sweater? Maybe you were afraid your sister would say no. Possible blind spot:

   - Your needs are more important than your sister's boundaries—you might tell yourself, "I'll put it back before she notices it's gone."

3. Why did you cheat to get the new account? You want the boss to see your value and earn more money. Possible blind spot:

   - Craving admiration and recognition, your inner dialogue might sound like, "I will do anything to maintain my leadership and monetary status."

PAUSE AND REFLECT:

Blind spots are the things we don't want to admit even to ourselves, so we justify, conceal, and deny them.

CONSIDER THIS:

How might blind spots show up when coaching around grief and trauma? By way of example, when responding to a client who recently miscarried, you might ask yourself why you answered with, "It's probably a blessing in disguise."

Your blind spot might be:

Looking on the bright side.

Or

Diminishing a topic you don't know how to resolve.

Or

Expressing your belief (instead of being curious about your client's experience).

PAUSE AND REFLECT:

What might your blind spot(s) be?

A WORD ABOUT THE INNER CRITIC

A close and noisier relative to the conscience is the inner critic—this is the voice that speaks up to stop us from doing something 'wrong' or 'bad,' or when we sense we've done something 'wrong' or 'bad' or when we worry about others' negative judgment.

Our inner critic evaluates our choices and chastises us when they don't align with its standards. This voice is loud and cruel; name-calling is a common trait. However, there's often a theme at the center of its insults; flawed, undeserving, failure, worthless, lazy, stupid, wrong, fraud, incompetent, weak, unlovable, fat, ugly—you get the picture.

The inner critic arrives when we are young to keep us out of trouble. After all, if we picked up all our toys, mom and dad didn't get mad at us. Unfortunately, it's impossible not to get in trouble once in a while when we're little, which feels horrible. So, the inner critic appeared to tell us what we did incorrectly or poorly so we could correct it before hearing a reprimand from our caretaker, teacher, or other adults. We began anticipating what needed doing and did our best to get it perfect, which awarded us praise but, more importantly, kept us from being told we were bad or flawed. The inner critic then took control of the judgment meter and worked to save us from heading toward the red.

CONSIDER THIS:

The inner critic works alongside our conscience, and together, they strive to keep us acting in alignment with their rubric. But unfortunately, even when we think the inner critic works to keep us honest and righteous, it is our puppet master. We may believe we act of our volition, but our motivation eventually becomes keeping the inner critic quiet.

PAUSE AND REFLECT:

Some people notice their inner critic as a heaviness or urgency in their belly or a harsh voice in their head, and for others, shame constricts their heart, making it hard to breathe. So, where does your inner critic make itself known within you?

THE INNER CRITIC AND COACHING

The inner critic gets such a stronghold on some of us that it eclipses our experiences, perceptions, and interactions. For many, looking for and noticing imperfections in oneself extends outward into seeing what's wrong or imperfect in the environment and others.

Bringing the inner critic to the coaching conversation, how might your inner critic surface when your client tells you they haven't completed their goal because the goal is too large? What if their reason for not meeting their goal is because their child recently shared that a family friend sexually abused them? Or because someone at the gym made a racial slur about them while standing next to their treadmill.

The first scenario about a goal that's too large has potentially elicited the client's inner critic—perhaps something for the coach to investigate. The second and third scenarios might tongue-tie a coach. In a moment of insecurity, your inner critic leaps in to remind you that you're a bad coach with commentary such as, "you should have had more training," "you're stupid and don't know what you're talking about," or, "this client knows you're incompetent."

CONSIDER THIS:

When you listen to your inner critic while in a coaching session, you're not coaching—you're not even present. When your inner critic begins its commentary, and you pay attention, your focus shifts from your client to yourself and your anxiety about competence, self-image, or saying the right or wrong thing.

PAUSE AND REFLECT:

What potential impact does your inner critic have on your coaching relationship?

PAUSING

What happens the first time we pause long enough to notice our inner witness? Maybe wonder, curiosity, or fear. Or perhaps we sense nothing. We'll probably unwittingly distract ourselves because we're much more comfortable focusing our attention outward than inward. However, coaches must possess the ability to look in both directions. Coaches need the ability to notice their distractibility and course-correct.

Pausing helps coaches ground themselves in a moment of distress, for example, when a client shares a traumatic experience like a sexual or physical assault. Taking a moment to pause and regain presence creates a sense of internal safety for your client. Likewise, when you're comfortable with silence and can wait before asking or answering a question, you demonstrate emotional stability for your client.

CONSIDER THIS:

Dr. Robert Kegan recommends using a consistent meditation practice that incorporates the inner observer to bring practiced objectivity to our patterned emotional reactions. Within this practice, he recommends imagining our thoughts, feelings, and urges as small objects to hold in the palm of our hand. He suggests that with this perspective, we can disconnect from our complicated thoughts and feelings and achieve a sense of peaceful solidarity with our fellow humans rather than our customary goal of individuality.

PAUSE AND REFLECT:

How might a coach use Bob Kegan's strategy while in a coaching session?

CONSIDER THIS:

Let's say a client tells you that they posted something private about you on their Facebook page. What's your emotional response? Panic? Fear? Shame? Embarrassment? You're unsure what to say or how to address this boundary breach. Furthermore, you're no longer present with your client at this moment of self-protection; you're thinking about the implications for yourself. Hopefully, you recognize that you must set aside your feelings before responding, but how?

Assuming you've met your inner witness through your meditation practice, you privately recognize and name your subjective experience; perhaps vulnerable, transparent, or exposed. Okay, you can work with that. Now, can you visualize whatever adjective you chose in the palm of your hand?

Next, try this; to yourself, quickly name the opposite of vulnerability (or whatever adjective you've chosen). What did you choose? Maybe confident, safe, or assertive?

Lastly, figuratively grab your opposing adjective and hold it in the palm of your other hand—now feel it, sense it. You've just made both vulnerability and its opposite objective and within your control. Make sense?

The final step is asking yourself how you might act or behave while feeling the second or opposing adjective [confident, safe, or assertive] and then **be** that.

PAUSE AND REFLECT:

By naming and holding the triggering adjective in the palm of your hand, and its opposing empowering adjective in your other hand, you're exerting control of your feelings and responding objectively, effectively removing yourself from your client's story.

CATEGORIES

What happens when we fortify this remarkable gift of our mind to observe versus subjectively evaluate or judge? We might begin to recognize the inherent ways we file everything and everyone into categories to make meaning out of every piece of information that passes through our mind's filter.

Using categories for our thoughts is efficient—if we didn't, our mental filing system would be atrocious! Indeed, our mind instinctively creates mental categories to develop meaning, certainty, predictability, and safety in a world that often feels confusing, uncertain, unpredictable, and unsafe.

How might coaches utilize the subjective data stored in their categories? First, coaches must become familiar with their categories to avoid labeling clients. With the help of our inner witness, we do this by noticing and halting our automatic evaluations—we stop our thoughts from sliding down a familiar neural pathway and instead create a new one.

Here's the fun part, when we recognize our automatic thought patterns, we can influence them. However, we can't change what we don't see, making inner witnessing vital to check assumptions that may inadvertently lead the coaching conversation where you want it to go rather than where your client wants to go.

For instance, we might design questions that validate our supposition based on our past experiences. If our mother died when we were young, we've categorized our feelings about that experience which may influence our response when our client tells us their mother died.

PAUSE AND REFLECT:

What's your category for people who wear Birkenstocks? Or people who drive Mercedes? What about someone addicted to heroin?

CONSIDER THIS:

And what about a category for a client's personality or preferences? I don't mean a mental health diagnosis, but a label or assumption based on a person's demeanor, appearance, or image—a client who straightens the magazines in your office or makes a joke about everything. How about a client who challenges nearly everything you say or one who often cries? Or a Christian, Atheist, or Buddhist?

PAUSE AND REFLECT:

What happens when you hear the above words and descriptions—what meaning is attached to them for you? First, you must recognize that these words merely represent concepts, and they do not fall into identical categories for every person.

HOW CATEGORIES HELP

As prey, we humans quickly learned our place in the food chain. We probably witnessed a lion attack a human, or perhaps our elders shared a story about lions eating humans for sustenance. So, to survive, when we see a lion, fear kicks in, and our mind puts "lion" in some version of a "danger" category. Do you see how our mind gets us from the visual "lion" to "fear" to the category "danger?" Right! Neural pathways! If humans were going to survive, we had to avoid predators. Once triggered, the 'danger' category sets the human in motion through a pre-determined neural pathway—fight, flight, or freeze (and faint or fawn).

Indigenous peoples lived entirely off the land and sea; they used canoes or catamarans for travel and fishing. They had no word or category for the ships the missionaries arrived on, nor for white people. Both indigenous and white people compared and categorized physical qualities, language, belongings, food, tools, and weapons. The missionaries seemed to have lumped the indigenous people into a "savages needing reform" category and treated them with abhorrent disrespect and arrogance. What category do you think the indigenous people might have had for the missionaries?

CONSIDER THIS:

Without an inner witness and conscious presence, our mind automatically and unconsciously categorizes and creates narratives for which we react as we always have, with clients and everyone else. Likewise, your clients are doing the same categorizing as you and about you.

FILES

Taking this one step further, once we recognize our categories, we can illuminate and index them in a brand new mental filing cabinet using curiosity and our inner witness!

Ever heard the quote "name it to tame it?" Coined by author and psychiatrist Dr. Dan Siegel, this phrase explains what happens when we shine a light on our categories. When we name the emotions that subjectively affect us, they lose their power and become objective. When our categories remain hidden from view, our opinions, intentions, and emotions run amok. When we bring them into the open, we can put our categories into a filing cabinet of our choice for later retrieval or recycling.

Categories and assumptions created over a lifetime reinforce our identity. Their contents can also elicit an intellectual, emotional, or physical response. As an example, while this varies from culture to culture, what goes through your mind when you hear 'Christmas tree?' This image conjures categories and assumptions, no matter the culture or religion, and for some, an emotional or spiritual sensation may arise.

You've probably not thought about where you store your assumptions about a Christmas tree; it's an automated system. Yet, your assumptions (beliefs) impact who you present to the world and influence how others experience you based on their assumptions. For example, if you wear a sweater embroidered with a Christmas tree, your client inherently puts you into a category that includes their beliefs about what a Christmas tree represents.

PAUSE AND REFLECT:

What is your automatic category (assumption) when told that someone's child died by suicide? What about when someone shares that they have seventeen cats and as many years of National Geographic magazines in their home? Or what about when your client tells you about their childhood abuse? How might your categories and assumptions impact your reaction in these cases?

CONSIDER THIS:

Imagine the category you've labeled 'Grief' just arose in a coaching conversation. What emotions are attached to this category for you? In other words, what assumptions do you make based on your categorization of grief? Perhaps pain, loss, emptiness, hurt, despair, loneliness, or dismay? What happens when something your client says springs open your grief category, tumbling all of your grief-associated feelings into your session? Do you begin to cry as your sorrow joins the conversation?

We remain impartial (objective) to our client's experiences when we're present, creating a safe space and empathic witnessing. However, when we're partial (subjective), we're lost in our story, accessing our categories and reacting accordingly—perhaps by changing the subject, identifying with our client's story, or attempting to problem-solve their experience.

NON-ATTACHMENT

As we've explored, the human mind wants to categorize, reinforcing assumptions and judgments. So, where and how does non-attachment support coaching within a mind that craves predictability?

Non-attachment begins outside the coaching session with non-evaluative, non-searching inner witnessing and awareness through regular practice. Non-attachment is the gift of a calm, peaceful coaching presence without a role or identity distraction. Non-attached coaching conversations start with open curiosity, letting the client choose the topic. It is receptive, curious coaching without agenda and welcoming to whatever energy or topic arises. Non-attached coaching is without a plan; instead, trusting in the coaching process. Non-attached coaching is knowing that we don't have the answers; our clients do—and we gladly embrace what they teach us.

Finally, non-attachment is a state of mind that completes conscious presence.

LIVING WITH GRIEF: DAY 37, CHANGE YOUR GREETING

Today is the thirty-seventh day Nicholas did not wake up.

I dreamt that Nicholas died just weeks before he did. One of those nightmares that feel real when you wake—the kind we dread and wonder if it means something. I was bothered enough by it to tell my closest friends. I remembered having this nightmare in the days after it became true.

Then, the week of Nicholas' death, I felt unnerved. Again, enough so that I told the people closest to me. I said I felt unsettled and knew I had felt that way since my dad died, but it was different, more intense, as though I was waiting for something terrible to happen. Again, I said I felt it in my gut, a disquieting knot; this too, I remembered in the days after Nicholas' death.

What does this mean? Am I crazy? Was I given a warning? Should I have done something to stop it? Was I somehow preparing myself for it?

The end remains the same.

And now we know. Nicholas died because of a bad batch of heroin cut with fentanyl. His intention was not to die; it was getting high, escaping. This knowledge doesn't change the outcome. Nicholas chose to roll the dice and lost.

He's not the only one.

In the last thirty-seven days, how many times have I heard "How are you?" Too many to count. If YOU had to guess, how do you think I am?

May I ask you something? How often do you want the truth when you ask this? How often do you ignore your audience while a mindless blurb exits your mouth because of conditioning?

I challenge you to change your greeting.

Earlier this week, I met with a client at the gym, and when he entered, he said, "morning." I was so relieved and grateful that "morning" was all I heard that I thanked him. It felt refreshing and thoughtful to hear "morning" instead of "good morning" or "how are you?"

Try this on for size: "It's nice to see you." There's more investment in it on your part, that's for sure. It's taking ownership of yourself and how the other person impacts you. Can you do this? Can you pay attention to the moment? Can you tell a person how you feel about seeing them rather than stating an empty inquiry?

How about in parting? Do you tell the other person to have a good day? Why? Have you ever thought about what you're saying? Do you believe YOU have that much control over another person to tell them what kind of day to have? Again, please think before ejecting words from your mouth. In Hawai'i, they say "Aloha," and in Ireland, they say "Cheers." What might you say instead of "Have a good day"?

Practice with me, please. Don't ask me how I'm doing. And don't tell me to have a good day. Instead, think about your audience and be present. Be intentional.

We all need to pay better attention.

IN CLOSING

Bringing together what we've talked about so far, the experience of grief spreads beyond the boundaries of death. Whether we're ready or not or think it's appropriate, grief, loss, and trauma will enter our coaching conversations because they're part of the human experience. Coaches must do their inner work or risk being ineffectual with these complex topics.

I challenge you to consider what's scary about sitting in the muck with your clients instead of looking for what's going well and setting SMART goals. What happens within *you* when your client uncovers a profound reason for their inability to stop eating ice cream at night—something a SMART goal can't overcome? How do you respond when your client doesn't achieve their goal because they can't find a reason to get out of bed? Sugar-coating or skirting the truth doesn't mean it's not there.

Your centering practice, combined with your coaching skills, prepares you for the messiness of being human. Use your exceptional human talent for self-reflection. With the help of your inner witness, discover the **who** beneath the image you project inward and outward—the *thinker*, *feeler*, *senser*, and *doer* within.

CLOSING INQUIRIES

You, your clients, and everyone in your life will benefit from a few minutes of your time spent in a presence practice each day. Not only are you changing the way you think, feel, and act, but how others, including your clients, experience you.

- *What are you willing to do to improve your coaching presence?*
- *What are some of your categories?*
- *How acquainted are you with your inner witness?*

*"Imagine the time it would take if every aspect of experience
had to be scrutinized afresh every minute of every day.
No. In order to free ourselves from the mundane,
it is essential that we delegate much of our interpretation
of the world to that lower area of the mind
that deals with the presumed, the assumed, the probable,
even though it sometimes leads us astray and causes us
to misinterpret a flash of sunlight as a girl in a white dress
when these two things are as unlike as two things can be."*

— Diane Setterfield, *The Thirteenth Tale*

PART 2

USING THE ENNEAGRAM

CHAPTER FOUR

SHOWING UP

"The path back to normal life is indescribably long
once death has swept the feet out from under those of us who are left.
Grief is a wild animal that drags us so far out into the darkness
that we can't imagine ever getting home again.
Ever laughing again. It hurts in such a way
that you can never really figure out
if it actually passes or if you just get used to it."

— Fredrick Backman, *Us Against You*

HABITS

We've covered a lot of ground, and now we're ready to take a deep dive into the habitual strategies we use to survive and, if we're lucky, thrive in our human lives.

We all employ various skills and wear suitable masks for managing our life experiences. Think back to your teenage years; a simple example is your behavior and appearance with your friends versus your parents versus at work or school. The people in our lives experience different versions of us based on what we want and allow them to see.

We've created strategic masks to assuage the emotional wounds sustained in our lifetime, but they limit our human potential. Hence, when we dismiss our emotional injuries, they persist and create interpersonal and intrapersonal difficulties. For coaches, not addressing our past wounds can impact our ability to coach impartially. Therefore, it is our responsibility to recognize our habitual emotional patterns so that we arrive at each coaching session with curiosity and without an agenda.

To begin learning our inner terrain, let's first notice how we humans have a habit of sorting almost everything bilaterally; good and bad, right and wrong, win and lose, pass and fail, all or nothing. If we hope to evolve as coaches and model self-development for our clients, this linear, polarizing language is limiting and unhelpful. Additionally, binary thinking and speaking bolster our inner critic, who loves to tell us we're fat (not thin), stupid (not smart), ugly (not attractive), loser (not a winner), etc., and not much in between.

Through training and experience, most coaches learn that we must consider our fundamental human *emotional*, *mental*, and *physical* health needs. Unsurprisingly, coaches sometimes strategize *nutrition*, *exercise*, and *sleep* with their clients for stress management, weight loss, and athletic performance. Recognizing there are three legs to consider to become a well-rounded person. Hopefully, coaches address with their clients that many long-term outcomes fall short when any of these three legs lag. In other words, focusing on just one or two elements of our fundamental self-development will eventually lead to frustration and collapse rather than growth and development.

TRIADS

For context:

A basic definition of a **triad** is *a group of three interconnected things or people.*

It's pretty easy to see the triad of *emotional, mental,* and *physical* health needs at work in our lives, and it's usually abundantly clear when one or more of these legs is broken or damaged. So, embracing the knowledge that humans are not two-dimensional, let's explore some triads that govern our lives, even if from backstage.

Self-Determination Theory is first on our list. This theory recognizes that *autonomy, relatedness,* and *competence* are psychological needs essential for moral human development and self-regulation. These three properties apply to all humans, including coaches and their clients, and impact our partnerships and development.

- *Autonomy* is the integrity we experience when our actions, thoughts, and feelings are self-regulated and authentic. In contrast, frustration arises when coerced or pressured to think, feel, or be something or someone we're not.

- *Relatedness* is the care, bonding, and love we experience when connecting with significant others. In contrast, we feel dismayed when excluded and socially isolated.

- *Competence* is feeling effective and masterful when utilizing our strengths and expertise. In contrast, aggravation indicates we feel inadequate and ineffective.

How you experience *autonomy, relatedness,* and *competence* affects how you interact with and interpret others, including your clients. For example, your coaching and your client will suffer if you're working with complicated topics like grief, loss, or trauma, and you fear that you lack *competence* in these areas. Alternatively, if mandated to coaching sessions, you'll probably see and sense your client's absence of *autonomy* need fulfillment.

When physically isolated, as with Covid-19, how might *your* need for relatedness influence a coaching relationship?

PRACTICAL USE OF TRIADS

As you can probably guess, perceiving our needs for autonomy, relatedness, and competence occurs with the help of our inner witness. Typically, we (figuratively) fall asleep to the patterns that govern our choices and actions—we run on autopilot rather than engage with the controls. For example, think about how you drive a car, probably without much presence since the activity is well patterned. Undoubtedly, driving with minimal presence is why and how car accidents occur. But, tragically, sleeping at the wheel is just how we spend our lives—with comfortable habits and familiar patterns rather than presence (remember, our mind likes predictability).

Fortunately, we can identify our three psychological needs in action by effortfully observing our daily patterns and habits. Unsurprisingly, it's easier to name and predict others' habitual patterns, like our children, who get defensive when asked to clean their room (shortage of *autonomy*).

Let's pretend a client shares with you that their spouse recently died in a car accident. Without any effort, you surmise that your client's sobbing suggests their psychological need for *relatedness* took a hit. So what do you choose to say? Conversely, what if your psychological need for *competence* gets triggered when you don't know what to say? In this case, rather than admitting you're at a loss for words or acknowledging their distress, you offer a platitude like, "I can't imagine what you must be going through, Client." You've successfully severed your connection with a statement that begins with "I can't"—precisely what could hurt your client most at that moment.

What happens when our primary psychological needs go unfulfilled or when we *believe* them to be unfulfilled? First, the mere possibility of unmet needs tangles us in our patterned thoughts, emotions, and reactions. And without *awareness*, our mind searches for and accesses the nearest analogous pathway to fulfill the psychological need's demand.

For instance, a coach might cross professional boundaries when *relatedness* at home is lacking while going through a divorce. Or, perhaps this same coach misreads a client's *relational* cues when presented with homemade cookies—a simple gesture of gratitude interpreted as romantic. In both cases, the coach's perceived (or not) unmet relatedness need induces a response that reinforces their patterned and habitual neural pathways.

Going back to our scenario with a client whose spouse died recently, let's assume that you do not recognize your client's injured need for *relatedness* and that you have no recognition that your need for *competence* exists. Your insecurity at that moment might cause you to fall into problem-solving, perhaps mimicking *competence*, and say something like, "It'll be important for you to keep your strength up in the coming weeks, let's brainstorm some ways to keep your stress level down." Yikes! There is no validation of your client's loss or their feelings. Instead, you've accomplished the swiftest path to *your* familiar ground thanks to well-worn neural pathways.

Yet, even with your habitual pattern fulfilled, you might feel uncomfortable because you missed the client's mark while attempting to fill your *competence* need. Why?

Returning to our client whose spouse died recently, this time, you observe that the tragic topic and your client's sobbing indicate they might feel a fissure in their need for *relatedness*. You also acknowledge that your insecurity spotlights a crater in your need for *competence*. On this occasion, while staying focused on your client, your response might be validating *relatedness* needs, "Oh, [Client]. You are safe here." This time, without effort or angst, choosing to address *relatedness*, you have simultaneously met your client's *relatedness* need and your need for *competence*.

A TRIAD OF CENTERS

Let's review a few ideas and then meet another triad that helps us uncover our psychological needs and how we tend to go about getting them met.

First, we all have neural pathways that reinforce habitual emotional and thought patterns for our psychological needs of relatedness, competence, and autonomy. Additionally, we know that our inner witness offers direct insight into these patterns and how they impact our coaching conversations and relationships.

And second, recall an introduction in Chapter 1 to a dynamic system poised for exploring your inner terrain called the Enneagram. In this chapter, we'll add a triad called the *Centers of Intelligence*, a foundational component of the Enneagram, offering further depth to perceiving human need satisfaction. These Centers of Intelligence are the **Heart Center** (or feeling center), the **Head Center** (or thinking center), and the **Belly Center** (or instinctive center).

WHAT IS THE ENNEAGRAM?

The Enneagram (pronounced ANY-a-gram) is a map to guide us to the *presence* we need to stay awake to life (and coaching) rather than sleeping through it. In addition, it sheds light on the habitual patterns we proficiently and unknowingly over-use (in other words, sleep) while attempting to meet our needs while deftly avoiding conscious presence.

With the help of an ancient diagram depicting nine numbers and interconnecting lines, the Enneagram dynamically illustrates and integrates our complex yet recognizable and strategic personality patterns. The Enneagram's inherent wisdom includes many triadic groups, including the Centers of Intelligence and another that we'll meet in the next chapter called the Harmonic Groups.

CENTERS OF INTELLIGENCE

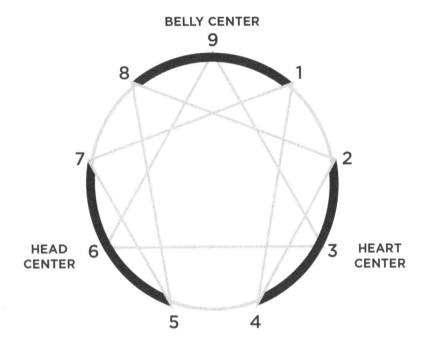

The Enneagram dates back as far as 2500 years in spiritual traditions, and more recently, in this century, modern psychology has begun adopting the Enneagram's insights. Furthermore, in keeping with today's diverse climate, the Enneagram does not discriminate or interfere with any chosen spiritual path, psychological approach, race, gender, sexuality, or nationality. Instead, the Enneagram's single purpose is to offer a direct but not simple route to conscious presence and our true nature.

To paraphrase a quote demonstrating the Enneagram's inherent value by Russ Hudson, one of the master teachers of the Enneagram and author of *The Wisdom of the Enneagram*, "The Enneagram brings awareness and presence to the patterns that run our lives most of the time. At its core, the Enneagram is a work of presence."

PERSONALITIES

Along with the three Centers of Intelligence, the Enneagram offers nine precise yet nuanced descriptions of our typical human personality characteristics. The personalities are the most recognized and discussed attribute of the Enneagram and, sadly, the most stupendously misinterpreted and applied.

For context:

WordNet 3.0 defines **personality** as: *the complex of all the attributes— behavioral, temperamental, emotional, and mental—that characterize a unique individual.*

Thus, *personality* is who and what we present to others, how we engage with the world, and how others perceive us.

First, however, understand that *we are not a personality type.* Accordingly, the nine numbers on the Enneagram diagram do not represent a distinct category in which we conveniently fit. For our purposes, I will correspond the numbers on the diagram to "*dominant biases*" to avoid the evaluations and limitations accompanying "type." Therefore, the nine dominant biases on the Enneagram diagram, represented by numbers, portray human attributes, tendencies, and patterns. The word I've chosen to denote each dominant bias and its corresponding number depicts a primary focus of attention.

CONSIDER THIS:

A personality structure is akin to temperament as defined in modern psychology. Dr. David Daniels (co-founder of The Narrative Enneagram training school) demonstrates a direct correspondence between the nine Enneagram personalities (dominant biases) and and the temperament styles of very young children described by Thomas and Chess in an NYU study spanning several years.

TRIADS AND THE THREE CENTERS OF INTELLIGENCE

Though we all have access to all three Centers of Intelligence, during our early years, we find that one Center of Intelligence best gets our needs met, and thus, we spend most of our time and energy there. Our dominant Center of Intelligence also becomes the primary lens for filtering and interpreting our experiences.

For context:

Center is defined as *an area that is approximately central within some larger region.*

While we are particularly sensitive to and identify with one Center of Intelligence, that does not imply it's a high point or forte; on the contrary, desiring predictability, our mind over-filters experiences through the Center of Intelligence that most resonate with us. Regrettably, over time, we limit and wound ourselves by spending too much time in one Center of Intelligence, much like we develop overuse injuries from sport overtraining and chronic disease from over-eating.

Additionally, our primary Center of Intelligence illuminates our principal method of *concealing* our habits and patterns from ourselves and others. With the neural pathways and habits we've created in our lifetime, we're blind to *why* we do what we do—without courageous introspection, we're mere puppets to our self-image (ego). Therefore, the three Centers of Intelligence are a starting point to discerning your barricades and obstacles to *conscious presence.*

CONSIDER THIS:

As coaches, it is our responsibility to continually self-assess with the help of our inner witness and through *conscious presence* to ensure we are always acting in the client's service, not ours. Therefore, our purpose here is to help you understand ***your*** Center of Intelligence while also utilizing *all three* Centers to return to *conscious presence* and provide what your client needs.

- The *Heart Center* focuses on and seeks to fill our need for *relatedness and emotional presence*.

- The *Head Center* focuses on and seeks to fill our need for *competence and present awareness*.

- The *Belly Center* focuses on and seeks to fill our need for *autonomy and physical presence*.

WHERE IT ALL BEGINS

From early childhood, we discover that the features of one of these three Centers of Intelligence most successfully fulfill our needs. Hence, we over-identify with and over-use that Center of Intelligence, making it our dominant Center of Intelligence.

Regrettably, a dominant Center of Intelligence limits our attention and experiences by narrowing our perceptual focus. Recall the neural pathways and habitual patterns that lead to predictable actions and reactions; in this case, over-using any single Center of Intelligence narrows our experiential lens.

So, for example, if the Heart Center is dominant, our (conscious or unconscious) attention is searching for validation through relating and connecting with others and receiving verbal and non-verbal feedback. In the case of the Heart Center, the feedback sought is in the form of attention, appreciation, recognition, and approval.

In contrast, if the Head Center is dominant, our attention focuses on our safety and security. In this case, attempts to keep fear and anxiety at bay will include planning, preparation, and information gathering.

And, if the Belly Center is dominant, our attention is on autonomy, self-reliance, and survival. Here, maintaining personal boundaries occurs through intuiting and reading the environment and imposing personal will.

Why are the Enneagram's Centers of Intelligence fundamental to the work of coaching? First, to understand that our clients most assuredly see and experience life differently from us, whether or not we share a dominant Center of Intelligence—we do not and cannot know our client's perspectives or interpretations of their experiences. Therefore, our purpose is to understand our dominant Center of Intelligence and how it interacts and interferes with our perceptions.

For example, if the Heart Center is dominant, our needs tend to over-focus on *relating* and might interfere with maintaining professional boundaries. So, again, recall the coach above with hazy boundaries and little insight into their divorce's impact on their *relatedness* needs—without awareness, that coach might attempt to fill their relatedness needs with a client.

THE ENNEAGRAM DIAGRAM AND ITS CENTERS OF INTELLIGENCE

The Enneagram diagram illustrates our three Centers of Intelligence, each containing three dominant biases that utilize strategies for securing and managing our human needs. Hence, each Center of Intelligence is a triad; the Heart Center triad, Head Center triad, and Belly Center triad (nine dominant biases and corresponding numbers in total). And as you already know, each Center of Intelligence has a kinship with the three Self-Determination Theory needs of *autonomy, relatedness, and competence*. These powerful triads clarify human behavior and reveal our fundamental challenges and asymmetries (the ways we lose *presence*), our intrinsic strengths and gifts, and our ability to self-reflect and be consciously present.

Noticing that the Centers of Intelligence and Self-Determination Theory's properties correspond with the three parts of the human brain; reptilian, limbic, and the neocortex, we can explore how each Center of Intelligence invites and undermines presence.

A. CENTERS OF INTELLIGENCE
B. SELF-DETERMINATION THEORY
C. THREE HUMAN BRAINS

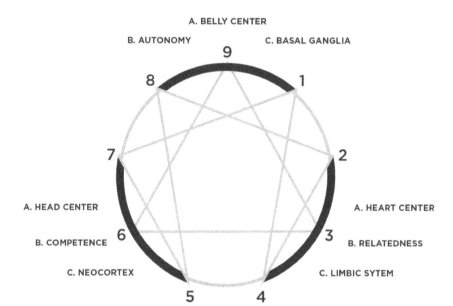

- The Heart Center relies upon attachment to and attention from others for survival. It corresponds with the *limbic system* or *emotional brain* and works to keep you connected (*relatedness*) with loved ones through affection and bonding. Striving for approval, validation, and recognition becomes the over-focused path to love and value. Yet, when we are present, the Heart Center offers the gift of **humanity**.

- The Head Center's job is to keep you safe and secure through knowledge and *competence*. Your *neocortex* or *rational brain* houses your higher intellectual qualities of discernment and wisdom. Over-focusing on unattainable assurance, stability, and predicting potential catastrophes causes considerable anxiety and insecurity. Yet, when we are present, the Head Center offers the gift of **clarity**.

- The Belly Center is your energetic, physical, and instinctive presence and corresponds to *autonomy* and the *basal ganglia* or *reptilian brain.* The reptilian brain aims to keep us alive and comfortable by intuiting the environment and determining the appropriate energy and action needed for survival. Habitually over-focused on personal volition, respect, and maintaining boundaries, *autonomy* eclipses organic presence. Yet, when we are present, the Belly Center offers the gift of **grounding**.

ENNEAGRAM TRIADS AND COACHING

CONSIDER THIS:

A new client shares a diagnosis you've never heard of, *nocturnal sleep-related eating disorder* (NS-RED). Your client believes it's essential that you know all of the facts to coach them properly and tell you the following story (they also share that they work with a therapist for depression and trauma): "I wake up after a couple of hours of sleep in an altered state, similar to being drunk, and I've eaten a full-size meal without memory of it; there's merely an empty plate with crumbs on it and an empty bag of chocolate sitting next to my bed as a clue."

PAUSE AND REFLECT:

What do you say to this client? First, pause and check in with yourself—what reactions do you notice?

Perhaps your **Heart Center** is dominant, so you know that emotions, connection, and validation are your default lens, and you rely on attention and approval from others to ensure your worth. So...

- Maybe your automatic reaction is to pretend that you've experienced NS-RED. For example, "That's happened to me, too, where I wake up with an empty quart of ice cream next to my bed, and I don't know where it came from."

In this example, *you believe that having the same experience bonds you.*

- Or maybe you immediately offer advice (which is not a coach approach). For example, "Would it work to put locks on your cupboards or fridge? If it's like you're drunk, combination locks might keep you out. Or maybe try an alarm on your bedroom door so it "wakes" you when you're having an episode?"

In this example, *finding efficient and practical solutions may award you recognition as an exceptional coach.*

- Or perhaps you ask more questions about their depression and anxiety. For example, "Wow, how disorienting, Client. What feelings come up when you talk with your therapist about this? Maybe we can explore those?"

In this example, *you believe that feelings are foundational, and the best coaching addresses painful experiences.*

A **Heart Center** alternative to all three of the above might be, *"What emotions arise for you, Client, as you share your experience of NS-RED with me?"*

In this example, you use your natural Heart Center ability to unveil feelings, something missing in your client's story, to help them connect with their emotional experience.

And what if your **Head Center** is dominant, where cognition and stability keep you secure?

- Maybe knowing nothing about NS-RED causes insecurity, so you fake your way through the session as though you have some expertise. "NS-RED is a cyclical illness—a cat and mouse game. Working on anxiety or depression awakens memories that increase the episodes, though ignoring the health consequences, causing further anxiety and depression."

In this example, *saving face in unfamiliar territory becomes more critical than maintaining empathy and connection with your client.*

- Or perhaps you fear your client's ability to overcome NS-RED and what that might mean for their life. "If you don't manage the NS-

RED, you are increasing your health risks. Plus, inadequate sleep negatively impacts your health. And driving it all is anxiety and depression. So you need to work on your mental health and make lifestyle changes to regain control of your life."

In this example, *your good intentions to avert anything worse from happening validates your perspective and invalidates your client's present experience.*

- Maybe you feel uncomfortable with what you see as a negative topic. It's not that you want your client to suffer, but their story doesn't sound like something within your scope, nor do you know anything about it. So, to lighten the energy between you, you might say, "What's the craziest thing you've eaten while sleeping? I wonder how you choose what to eat when you're sleeping?"

In this example, *your redirection leaves your client feeling dismissed and confused.*

A **Head Center** alternative to all three of the above might be, *"What have you learned about yourself since receiving the NS-RED diagnosis, Client?"*

Your keen Head Center curiosity helps bring awareness and synthesis to your client's diagnosis in this example.

This time your **Belly Center** is dominant, where maintaining your energetic boundaries and earning respect through personal will supports your *autonomy*.

- You're having a hard time knowing how to respond because you want to tell your client to decide to wake up when an episode begins and then do it. "While it takes some work, we can wake up from our dreams with determination. So with some effort on your part, I bet you can wake up before heading to the kitchen."

In this example, *you're troubleshooting and perhaps even projecting inhibits empathy.*

- Or you might identify with the ability to lose yourself, your sense of time, and feeling unsurprised that an entire bag of popcorn can disappear without tasting it. Yet you prefer to remain unruffled by an unfamiliar topic. "It might seem scary being out of control, yet nothing is permanent. If you stop worrying about it for a while, maybe it'll resolve itself."

In this example, *identifying with the topic causes you to retract and emotionally minimize your client's experience with friendly advice.*

- Lastly, you're frustrated with your client's inability to take responsibility for what they eat. Yet, you see a clear solution, and you're ready to strategize. "Step one is not purchasing excess or unhealthy food. If it's not in the house, you can't eat it."

In this example, *judgment and problem solving overshadow acknowledging your client's struggle.*

A **Belly Center** alternative to all three of the above might be, *"How do you experience yourself as you consider what you've just shared, Client?"*

Using your innate Belly Center capacity for presence, you've invited your client to perceive themselves in real-time.

OVERUSE

While we use and have access to all three Centers of Intelligence, we get stuck using one predominant center thanks to reinforcement through our neural pathways. In other words, we create a dominant filter (bias) through which we observe and experience the world and seek to fulfill our needs.

If the Heart Center (*relatedness*) is your dominant filter and *feelings* are its need fulfillment approach, you liberally use emotional connection to meet your psychological needs. However, with overuse, connecting becomes manipulative and harrowing. As an illustration, if *relatedness* is a coach's dominant bias, they might cry upon hearing a sorrowful client story, overshadowing their client's experience and blurring the coach/client boundary.

Suppose the Head Center (*competence*) is your dominant filter with thinking as its need fulfillment bias. In that case, you might liberally use ideas, knowledge, and possibility to meet your psychological needs. However, these things become scrutiny, insecurity, and escapism with overuse. In this example, with an over-focus on fulfilling a need for competence, this coach may feel inferior and anxious about a complicated and unfamiliar topic during coaching sessions.

And if the Belly Center (*autonomy*) is your dominant filter, where *physical and energetic regulation* satisfies psychological need fulfillment, you liberally use personal will to meet your psychological needs. However, with overuse, energy and grounding become control, anger, and avoidance. Therefore, if a coach's dominant bias is *autonomy*, they might maintain a firm, energetic boundary to avoid risking transparency, ineptitude, and emotional drain, thus extinguishing the possibility of trust and rapport.

WHAT MAKES THESE CENTERS INTELLIGENT?

Intelligence does not mean wise here but innate. Our mind eagerly scans for affirming experiences, reinforcing our dominant Center's Intelligence or convictions. Each Center's 'Intelligence' functions to protect our basic and psychological human needs, using rudimentary and predictable emotions to regain equilibrium when threatened.

CONSIDER THIS:

Our purpose here is to help you become familiar with your dominant Center of Intelligence so that you can enlist the other two Centers of Intelligence more readily. Knowing your client's dominant Center of Intelligence isn't necessary; knowing yours is what's important. When you recognize the Center of Intelligence that most resonates with you, you'll understand how and why you relate to your clients and their experiences as you do. Then, with insight rather than habit, you can choose your responses rather than your patterned reactions.

EMOTIONS

Unsurprisingly, specific emotions correspond with each Center of intelligence and evoke predictable reactions when triggered. In *The Enneagram Journal*, "Toward the Neurobiology of the Enneagram" (July 2009), Jack Killen's article demonstrates and enhances our understanding of emotion regulation corresponding to each Center of Intelligence.

Shame and *distress* motivate the Heart Center. Experiencing disconnection, disruption, or invalidation within relationships alights the Heart Center with **distress** and **shame**, thereby initiating strategies to regain connection, attention, validation, and *relatedness*.

Anxiety and *fear* incite the Head Center. Feeling unstable, threatened, or insecure, the Head Center endures **fear** and **anxiety** while initiating a hunt for security, certainty, stability, and *competence*.

Anger and *rage* impel the Belly Center. When feeling violated, disrespected, or treated unjustly, the Belly Center adapts with **anger** and **rage** and urges the restoration of order, justice, respect, and *autonomy* with sheer will and volition.

MISMATCHED CENTERS

PAUSE AND REFLECT:

Imagine your Belly Center is dominant, governed by anger and rage, and seeking *autonomy*. Yet, your client's Heart Center is dominant, managed by distress and shame, and in pursuit of *relatedness*. In this case, you may feel outraged and an urge to protect your client when they tell you about their stolen three-month-old beagle puppy, George. In contrast, your client feels tormented and tearful about their lost companion and the ensuing disconnection from their missing loved one. Suppose you, the coach, lack self-insight in this scenario. In that case, you might react with your Belly Center's innate emotional patterns (anger and rage) and miss the mark on your client's need for emotional connection.

Or let's say your client learns they need a kidney transplant and dialysis until that happens. This time, your Heart Center (*relatedness*) is dominant while your client's Head Center (*competence*) is dominant. In this example, you feel distressed hearing their shocking news because you don't want your client to suffer, and you don't want to lose your coach/client relationship. With a dominant Head Center, you want to do something to help your client feel cared for, so you try intently to connect with them through feelings to get a sense of what you can do. Meanwhile, your client, who experiences this news through the Head Center, is anxious and afraid of what comes next. Your client wants guidance while trying to make sense of this unwanted and uncertain situation. They long to regain a sense of certainty and predictability but don't know how to do it. Meanwhile, you're trying to connect emotionally to meet your needs rather than meeting the client where they need you.

CONSIDER THIS:

Focusing on your client's potential dominant Center of Intelligence is not the objective—you need to know your dominant Center of Intelligence to remain open and present and access all three Centers of Intelligence. Our aim in this book is self-insight—*powerful coaching always starts with ourselves.*

THE LAY OF THE LAND

Let's talk about the layout and value of the Enneagram diagram for a moment. Why? Because the Enneagram diagram brings to life often complex reactions—from mere psychology to eccentric spirituality. While the Enneagram diagram is not complicated, it may seem like an enigma at first glance, and I'd like you to have some understanding of its practicalities. However, because we're exploring relatively few aspects of the Enneagram, my explanation will be as uncomplicated as possible.

Henceforth, we'll move beyond the Enneagram's Centers of Intelligence and explore each of the nine dominant biases depicted on the diagram with numbers. Our exploration is getting more nuanced to help you locate and understand the dominant bias that most resonates with you. And, in turn, escorting you closer to *conscious presence*.

As you delve into self-observation a bit more (with the help of your inner witness) and learn to put the Enneagram to practical use in coaching conversations (and life), you might find learning more about and referencing the Enneagram diagram beneficial if not curious.

ENNEAGRAM DIAGRAM

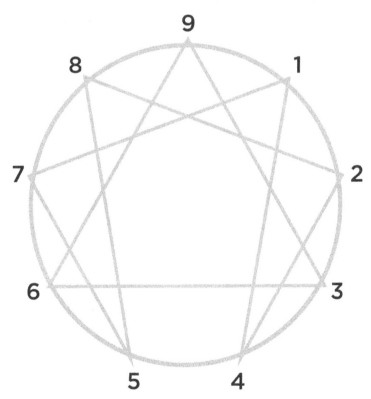

CONSIDER THIS:

The Enneagram diagram is not static but a dynamic, revealing map of human personality patterns, how they limit our potential, and how to break free, thus delivering us to *conscious presence*. Its design includes a deliberate sequence of numbers on an outer circle connected by intentional inner lines.

Additionally, you'll notice an equilateral triangle connecting numbers 3, 6, and 9. These three numbers fall in the middle of their respective Centers of Intelligence, and each has two flanking numbers—for example, numbers 2 and 4 flank number 3.

The 3, 6, and 9 are "Primary" because they represent the dominant biases most stuck in their habitual patterns within their Center of Intelligence. In other words, untangling the challenges of these three dominant biases is most complex.

As you can see, numbers 1, 4, 2, 8, 5, and 7 are intentionally connected by lines forming a hexad and flank the 3, 6, and 9 on the equilateral triangle.

Numerals 1, 4, 2, 8, 5, and 7 are "Secondary" because their dominant biases are more yielding and versed, though no less complicated to untangle.

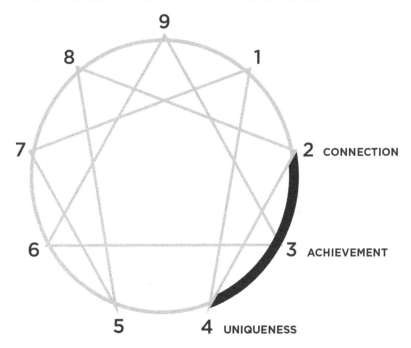

HEART CENTER AND ITS THREE DOMINANT BIASES

THE HEART CENTER AND ITS EMOTIONAL INTELLIGENCE

The Heart Center's predominant focus is **emotions** and contains numbers 2, 3, and 4.

- With a dominant bias of **Connection** at number 2, positive feelings get overexpressed while repressing negative *emotions*.

- As the Heart Center's primary number, 3 is the most estranged from their feelings in favor of productivity and appearing outstanding in others' eyes with a dominant bias toward **Achievement**.

- Emotional expression is the least developed at number 4, with a dominant bias toward **Uniqueness**. Rather than straightforward diction, mused feelings are shared obscurely through aesthetics and drama.

Those who resonate with the Heart Center have an emotional filter, experiencing and interacting with emotional intelligence. These folks have a dynamic emotional radar and tune into others' emotions and temperaments. Once sensing the emotional state of others, they strive to connect, thus receiving validation and approval. Recognition from others is their principal origin of self-esteem, connection, and love. Reading another's emotional state allows the ability to mirror emotional needs through an adaptable personal image, ensuring validation, approval, and *relatedness*.

People whose dominant bias is in the Heart Center mistakenly believe their self-image or self-designed facade to be their true identity. In reality, their self-image is an ego-driven imitation created to elicit validation from anywhere but within themselves.

CONSIDER THIS:

Without affirmative mirroring from caregivers when they were small, self-representation became essential to avoid the *shame* of being insignificant for those whose Heart Center is dominant. Validation became a life-support system with *shame* and *distress* lurking beneath the surface; for who are they without an affirmation of their worth and devoted connection? *Shame* can trigger panic and hostility, and only attention and connection can restore relationships and equilibrium.

THE HEART CENTER'S POSITIVE CONTRIBUTIONS INCLUDE:

Responsiveness, altruism, connection, achievement, drive, adaptability, benevolence, efficiency, creativity, authenticity, and elegance.

HEAD CENTER AND ITS THREE DOMINANT BIASES

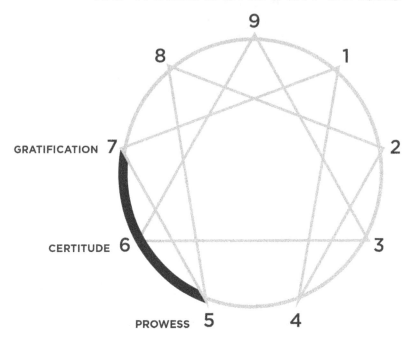

THE HEAD CENTER AND ITS COGNITIVE INTELLIGENCE

The *Head Center's* predominant focus is **thinking** and comprises numbers 5, 6, and 7.

- With a dominant bias of **Prowess** at number 5, *thinking* gets overdeveloped with the private immersion of concepts and ideas taking the place of action.

- As the Head Center's primary number, 6 is the most disconnected from their thinking faculties. With a dominant bias toward **Certitude**, rumination about possible actions while doubting their ideas and insights becomes a substitute for taking action.

- With a dominant bias of **Gratification** at number 7, rudimentary thinking fuels endless loops of abandoned ideas and disregarded intentions while emphasizing novelty, anticipation, and pleasure.

The primary focus is on assuaging *anxiety* and uncertainty through planning, data gathering, and strategizing for those whose Head Center is dominant. There's a lot of mental chatter about the dangerous world we live in; hence, a dominant Head Center lends itself to spending a lot of energy thinking. The constant gibber is both soothing and troubling; folks who most resonate with the Head Center feel most comfortable within their minds yet struggle to find the best solution for living. As a result, copious amounts of time get spent researching, planning, visualizing, anticipating, and ruminating in hopes of finding sound guidance while avoiding the unexpected and instability.

Folks who resonate with the Head Center are prone to 'analysis paralysis' while attempting to create a sense of safety, security, and stability. Planning, preparation, and information gathering are habitual anxiety relief strategies; still, uncertainty and fear loom despite their vigilance.

CONSIDER THIS:

As small children, folks whose Head Center is dominant lacked the appropriate guidance necessary when testing independence, fostering fear and insecurity in their ability to keep themselves safe and secure. Quieting the mind through presence is the antidote for fear and anxiety and the source of certainty and competence.

THE HEAD CENTER'S POSITIVE CONTRIBUTIONS INCLUDE:

Expertise, curiosity, innovation, loyalty, caution, discernment, enthusiasm, spontaneity, focus, imagination, and guile.

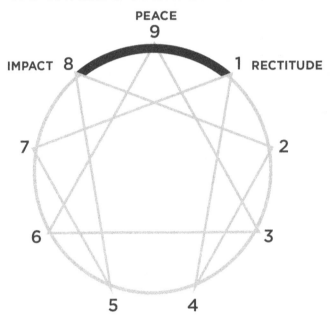

BELLY CENTER AND ITS THREE DOMINANT BIASES

THE BELLY CENTER AND ITS SOMATIC INTELLIGENCE

The Belly Center's predominant focus is **instinct** and houses numbers 8, 9, and 1.

- With a dominant bias of **Impact** at number 8, taking action before considering the consequences illustrates overexpressed *instincts*.
- The Belly Center's primary number, 9, is the most out of touch with their instincts. To remain internally undisturbed, disengaging from the discomfort of human life fulfills a dominant bias of **Peace**.
- Underdeveloped instincts result from a dominant bias of **Rectitude** at number 1. Irritation and rigid standards become catalysts while simultaneously repressing instinctual drive.

Experiencing life from a Belly Center perspective includes a kinesthetic knowing, a 'gut feeling.' The people who have this visceral experience are probably those telling us, "trust your gut!" However, this intuitive and physical sensation can also bestow warnings and predictions if one is inclined to receive these messages.

People who resonate with the Belly Center have an often notable propensity for nature and Mother Earth. Curiously, they may seem firmly planted on the ground or barely touching it. Compare a Sumo wrestler awaiting the start of a match, solid and unmovable, firmly planted in their center of gravity, with someone sitting in meditation, eyes closed and peaceful, appearing as subtle as a levitating Buddha. Although if you pay close attention, both seem intimately connected to the earth.

Autonomy, the Belly Center's primary focus, includes owning its physical space; like an old cedar tree rooted in the soil, *grounding* may come naturally.

Just as feelings originate in the Heart Center and thoughts occur in the Head Center, sensations arise in the Belly Center. And while thoughts journey to the future and feelings muse the past, our physical body can be nowhere but right here, right now. Accordingly, the Belly Center is where we connect with our power, immediacy, and *presence*.

CONSIDER THIS:

As small children, those whose Belly Center is dominant didn't experience the freedom of youth; instead, they became little adults to manage environmental pressures. Their constraints unsurprisingly lead to an *angry*, *rageful* resistance. As adults, physical, emotional, or mental encroachment invites aggravation, resulting in a declaration of power through *anger* and vehement boundary-setting. Securing their position on this earth is job number one for those dominant in the Belly Center, as both *autonomy* and volition lead to integrity, assurance, and respect.

THE BELLY CENTER'S POSITIVE CONTRIBUTIONS INCLUDE:

Wisdom, integrity, morals, harmony, tolerance, confidence, protection, leadership, peacefulness, acceptance, and impartiality.

WHAT'S NEXT?

In the next three chapters, we'll explore the Enneagram's nine dominant biases in more detail and directly correlate each with another powerful Enneagram triad called the Harmonic Groups. The safe space created within the coaching relationship depends on our emotional intelligence. The Harmonic Groups reveal how we, as coaches, might inadvertently interrupt the coaching process when we aren't *consciously present*, have an agenda, or get emotionally triggered. The Harmonic Groups also provide foolproof strategies for keeping your client front and center even with discomforting topics.

CONSIDER THIS:

A brief history of the Harmonic Groups: Russ Hudson discovered three modalities for resolving conflict or challenges within our relationships, which, unsurprisingly, occurs when we feel deprived of our wants.

Accordingly, within each of these three modalities are three dominant biases. Or, to put it another way, there are three frustration reaction strategies split equally among the nine Enneagram dominant biases.

Finally, the three Harmonic Groups describe the three predictable ways we fuel continued disharmony while attempting to get our needs met and how to end the nonsense.

LIVING WITH GRIEF:
DAY 49, WILL YOU IMAGINE IT?

If I were going to torture someone, I would set them in my shoes. Tragically, I am sure that this year's events are an evil spell cast by someone who hates me.

Do you know what it's like to do nothing but rearrange pictures and new albums, endlessly searching for the perfect frame for hours? Do you know that it's never enough? Being unable to do anything but try to bring back the unappreciated security that your children are living is exhausting and fruitless.

Are you able to imagine the unreality of looking at your child's photo, REMEMBERING how you felt when it was new, and the infinite love and despair of knowing there will never be another? Will you imagine it? Will you sit with me while I am IN it?

Please don't tell a parent who has lost a child that you are sorry for their loss or can't imagine what we're going through. This experience is MINE, and those who have lived it, do not make it about you because it is not.

Please don't tell me it's going to get better, that I will get through this, that time will heal me. YOU don't know these feelings or how long they will last, and you probably never will - unless you have, and in that case, please share your pain with me.

For the rest of you, try just sitting with me in my pain and don't run away.

IN CLOSING

While learning about the Enneagram, I invite you to arrive with curiosity and receptivity as you learn about your dominant bias and how you might develop—in contrast to mere fascination and the opportunity to "type" yourself and everyone you know. Remember, the Enneagram is a map for *self-discovery* and *self-development* that includes a path to our conscious presence—it is not a tool or toy for branding people.

CONSIDER THIS:

We all possess all nine of the Enneagram dominant *biases* or personality structures. The trouble is that we become blind to our singular overuse—yet another of our habitual patterns. When we recognize our dominant bias or dominant personality pattern, the possibility of seeing our blind spots and our many strengths opens.

This book aims to help you understand yourself more intimately, enabling you to return to *conscious presence* and provide what your client needs. It's our responsibility to continually self-assess to ensure we're always acting in the client's service, not our own, with the help of our *inner witness*.

But, remember, embarking on genuine change takes courage and perseverance because our ego (personality) attempts to thwart every effort with self-bolstering, biases, and tendencies.

This book is a springboard for self-exploration and is nowhere near a complete picture. Nonetheless, the information may be emotionally triggering for some people at times. Should that happen, I invite you to set down the book and return to it when it feels safe.

CLOSING INQUIRIES

Next, we'll explore each dominant bias within its Harmonic Group so that you might identify the strategies most familiar to you and uncover how you get in the way of your best coaching and, finally, how to recover your presence.

Remember, building the essential inner scaffolding for clambering behind your *dominant biases* begins with a daily presence practice.

- Which Center of Intelligence do you experience as most familiar?

- Which psychological need do you most identify with; *relatedness*, *competence*, or *autonomy*?

- Which primary emotion feels most unfamiliar to you; *shame*, *fear*, or *anger*?

*"Do you remember the tiny curl of your fingers,
the dimples on the backs of your hands in that first year of your life?
The complete contemplation in those fingers
as they wrapped around mine.
Hours of your frogged arms and legs against my chest,
both of us deep in sleep. Your downy cheek against mine.
Now we are on our knees, your father, brother, and me,
and we place the lei in the pit,
and the soil slides back over it like an eyelid closing
that will never open again."*

— Kawai Strong Washburn, *Sharks in the Time of Saviors*

CHAPTER FIVE

THE POSITIVE OUTLOOK HARMONIC GROUP

"Two things I thought about: First, you are like an amputee,
a part of you is gone, but you will always remember
it was a part of you, and second, you do not have to think
about how awful the next ten years will be.
You just need to decide to get up tomorrow
and then the next day and the next."

— Joanne Grimsrud

PERSONALITIES AND HARMONIC GROUPS

At this point, I hope you are beginning to grasp how understanding the Enneagram can help you in a coaching context. Quite simply, it can provide a wealth of knowledge if you are willing to do the work of self-exploration. It is only through inner witnessing and courage that we are able to choose to come back again and again to conscious presence when faced with difficult topics in the coach-client relationship.

To begin, let's turn our attention to the Enneagram's nine dominant biases within their respective Harmonic Groups and how this information can impact and improve our coaching, but first, a bit more context about the Harmonic Groups.

Each Harmonic Group reveals a patterned approach to challenging topics or personal and professional conflicts. Unfortunately, our triggers and responses can be obscure and are most often mismatched with the patterned defense system of the other person—generating dissonance. So if a client says or does something that triggers us, we undeniably respond in a manner aligned with one of these Harmonic Groups.

As coaches, our goal is to recognize our primary Harmonic approach and learn how to enact the other two when needed. Consequently, as we broaden our methods, we mirror practical, affirming, and authentic conflict resolution strategies with our clients.

HARMONIC GROUPS

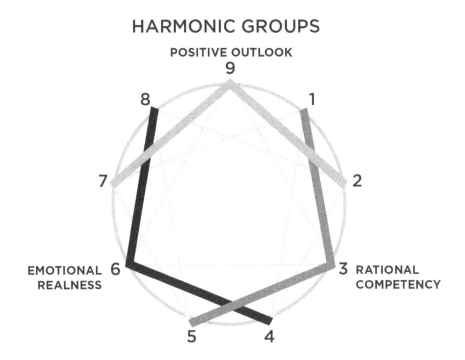

Keep in mind that each Harmonic Group has three subtle variations, depending on the particular dominant bias in question. Chapters 5, 6, and 7 address each of the three Harmonic Groups and their dominant biases with easy-to-follow, detailed characterizations.

Chapters 5, 6, and 7 include a brief introduction to the Harmonic Group's orientation, followed by four first-hand narratives for you to "try on" so that you can explore which most resonates with you.

After the four first-hand narratives, you'll find four third-person practical segments applicable to your work as a coach as you work with the Harmonic Groups.

Each segment closes with a developmental breathing practice specific to that dominant bias and its Center of Intelligence and Harmonic Group. This breathing practice can be your daily presence practice and is immensely helpful when you feel emotionally triggered. Finally, after the breathing practice, there are dominant bias-specific insights and an inquiry to expand your self-awareness.

We begin with the Positive Outlook Harmonic Group and will address the Rational Competency Harmonic Group in Chapter 6, and finally, the Emotional Realness Harmonic Group in Chapter 7.

THE POSITIVE OUTLOOK HARMONIC GROUP

DIAGRAM NUMBERS 9, 2, 7

The Positive Outlook Harmonic Group focuses on what's positive in life and actively avoids negative experiences and emotions. Though each dominant bias has a unique twist on maintaining a positive attitude, their demeanor emanates positivity. The Positive Outlook approach includes reframing unpleasant feelings positively through affirmation, encouragement, and bolstering. And while they have genuine goodwill for humanity, confronting problems, facing distressing emotions, and addressing their needs and the needs of others become asymmetrical. As a result, they sometimes view others as too negative. For the folks dominant in the Harmonic Positive Outlook patterns, distraction and avoidance happen through humor, redirection, withdrawal, aloofness, caretaking, and denial.

PAUSE AND REFLECT:

Observe how these dominant biases resonate with you as you read through these three descriptions. Do you see yourself in any of these descriptions? Can you relate to any of these dominant biases? This inner witnessing is the beginning of your exploration.

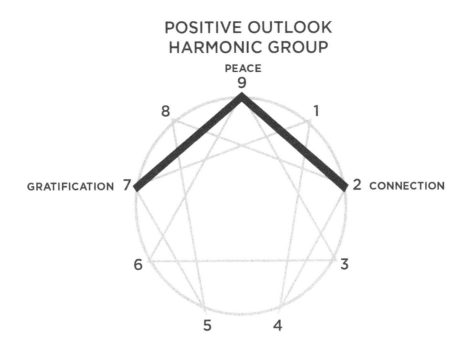

DOMINANT BIAS:
PEACE, DIAGRAM NUMBER: 9

I enjoy deep conversations, taking in what others say with interest. I quickly put people at ease and hope to maintain a connection with them. I want others to value me, and I want to feel seen and heard, though I'd never say that aloud. I'm genuinely curious about people and enjoy hearing their stories. I sometimes need time to formulate my interests, position, and insights, and I appreciate your patience as I take time to form my thoughts into words.

I value harmony, maintain a sense of comfort, and try not to rock the boat. And, of course, I appreciate it when you don't rock the boat either. So while I might have strong opinions, I've put them on the back burner so as not to disturb the peace. However, if I have a firm conviction, you'll hear it—it just doesn't happen often.

If you ask me what I want to do or where I'd like to go, I'll likely say, 'I don't know; wherever you want to go is fine.' And if you push me for an answer, the inquisition will cause me to withdraw, though not necessarily physically. I'm a master at hiding in my imagination.

I enjoy activities in which I can lose myself: reading, knitting, working, and binge-watching Netflix, though these activities can also become my Achilles heel. I'm easily distracted and prone to inertia, so tasks sometimes take longer than they ought. In addition, I tend to procrastinate activities that produce anxiety or anger, like replying to a confrontational email, paying overdue bills, or making a return of something purchased but no longer wanted.

I'm surprisingly disconnected from my physical being and have difficulty sensing experiences; exercise, for example. To tell you where I have sensations while doing a squat might be impossible because I'm escaping the workout's discomfort to the comfort of my mind. I don't want to be present and feel physically uncomfortable—what a relief when the exercise is over! It seems I'm either in my body or my head, but not often simultaneously. In other words, presence can be challenging for me.

Because I sometimes feel insignificant and invisible, I silently doubt that people hear me when I speak, making me prone to over-explaining and over-telling. I want to be sure my point gets across, and when it's important to me, I can mistakenly talk over others and get stubborn.

Contrary to feeling invisible, sometimes I feel pressured to have a viewpoint or make a decision, which alights my anger. So in those times, I clam up and refuse an opinion, which makes others think I'm indecisive or ambivalent. The thing is, I often don't have a strong opinion, and I don't want one, so when I feel cornered to state an opinion or make a decision, I shut down and check out.

HOW I WANT YOU TO PERCEIVE ME

Calm, agreeable, supportive, unbiased, receptive, flexible, easygoing, friendly, inclusive, amiable, consistent, and tolerant.

MY COACHING STYLE

I effortlessly focus on my clients, instilling safety and openness. I hope to inspire serenity and wisdom through my coaching. My style is curious and unbiased, and I enjoy learning about people through their stories. My patience and silence allow feelings and thoughts to come forth in due time. A cornerstone of my coaching is supporting others in discovering their obstacles and accomplishments to create a whole and autonomous person. I love championing my clients and celebrating their achievements and strengths.

The duality of presence and absence is one of my challenges, not physically but emotionally and energetically. Conflict or other uncomfortable topics can send me out of the room, metaphorically speaking, especially if it involves me. A worst-case scenario is falling asleep while a client is talking. Also, because I prefer serene, peaceful stories, I sometimes allow a session to go off-topic while lost in a fanciful tale, leading to another problem; uncertainty about my role.

WHAT I AVOID

Conflict, or its possibility, triggers my habit of avoiding reality. I'll energetically disappear though you'll only notice complacency and resignation. Sometimes I feel as though what I want doesn't matter, making me feel invisible, unworthy, and unable to say 'no.' And feeling insubstantial can bring up rage, which is terribly uncomfortable for me. But, ultimately, I'd rather be what you want than risk alienation. So rather than speak directly and honestly for fear of losing our connection, I'll act out passive-aggressively, withdraw my attention, and escape to my mind.

POSITIVE OUTLOOK

People whose dominant bias is **Peace** prefer comfort and harmony and employ a few strategies to shift their attention when anger or discomfort arises. One approach might be reframing their outlook until they don't see a problem. Another might be turning their attention to something more pleasant (reframing reality) until rage subsides, which might include telling themselves and others, 'This too shall pass.' Finally, avoiding anger and conflict might be described as 'sticking their head in the sand' or 'checking out' by those close to or dealing with someone who resonates with the dominant bias Peace.

HOW THIS MIGHT SHOW UP IN COACHING

Without self-awareness, preferring comfort and feeling unbothered may get in the way of conscious presence, objectivity, and empathy. For example, feeling overwhelmed with others' energy and needs, a coach whose bias is Peace may secretly withdraw to the comfort of their mind when their energy runs low. Additionally, with an objective not to rock the boat, this coach may not challenge a client when it would help them move forward. Instead, a coach whose bias is Peace might redirect uncomfortable topics which may inadvertently feel dismissive or invalidating to a client.

A SCENARIO

Your client arrives in a flurry of anger and despair and shares that someone broke into their house, destroyed property, and stole valuables. Your client feels traumatically violated, afraid, and despondent. You know that this conversation will not be the usual goal review and goal setting, and the topic and heightened emotional energy cause you discomfort. You sense your client as out of control and have no idea what to say, yet you feel their eyes on you expectantly. You feel backed into a corner, which triggers anger, and you begin to retreat; you lean away from your client to create distance. Your client sees and feels your withdrawal and closes the physical distance between you. You sense the client's attempt to usurp all of your energy, so you escape to the safety of your imagination and leave just enough energy to sit still and appear present with few words until your session is over.

BREATHING PRACTICE FOR DOMINANT BIAS PEACE

Breathing is the fastest and most reliable way to return to presence, and particular dominant biases benefit from specific breathing practices. The following breathing practice is adapted from the work of Russ Hudson and Jessica Dibb in their program, *The Enneagram in Conscious Living*.

First, find a comfortable yet alert position in which to sit (you may also do this breathing practice while standing). Then, with your eyes open in a gentle gaze, bring your attention to your belly. Keep both hands on your lap, palms down, or one hand on your stomach, laying your other hand palm down in your lap. Breathe deeply through your nostrils, allowing first your stomach and then your rib cage to expand. Hold your breath in for a moment before exhaling slowly through your nostrils. Feel the relaxation of your chest, rib cage, and belly. Take a brief pause before beginning your next inhale. Remember James Redfield's maxim, "where attention goes, energy flows," and keep visualizing your breath as a wave that travels down to your Belly Center and then up, expanding and raising your chest cavity.

This breathing exercise is suitable when you notice yourself energetically withdrawing to avoid discomfort and as a daily practice.

Do this as a daily practice to:

- Access immediate grounding when activated.
- Recognize and acknowledge your repressed rage.
- Accept suffering as a part of human life.
- Develop neural pathways to conscious presence.

Practice noticing and naming what triggers the initiation of your energetic withdrawal. This predictable retreat indicates hidden rage and protects against energy depletion and your difficulty with boundary setting. Though counterintuitive, anger and rage affirm your presence and value and provide the energy required to verbalize your needs, set limits, and stand up for yourself.

A DEEPENING AWARENESS INQUIRY FOR DOMINANT BIAS PEACE

Who are *you* at 100% present?

DOMINANT BIAS: CONNECTION, DIAGRAM NUMBER: 2

I love people! I love seeing people happy and fulfilled. My world centers around ensuring the people in my life are well-cared for and know that they can come to me for anything at any time. What I have is yours, and if I don't have it, I'll cheerfully get it for you. I love hosting events and parties, and I'm fantastic at it! Preparing an environment and the food that makes friends and family feel loved, enriched, and at ease makes me happy.

One thing that's difficult for me is taking care of myself. It's uncomfortable to consider what I need and want, and I feel better about myself by taking care of you. I have endless energy and use it all in the service of others. I'm an expert at predicting what you want and need and will get it for you before you recognize or verbalize that something is missing. I pride myself on my selflessness and natural ability to take excellent care of others. For example, if you need a tray of caramel rolls at your 7:00 a.m. gym class, I will get up at 4:00 a.m. to make two batches, one without nuts and the other with nuts (yes, an oxymoron to bring caramel rolls to the gym, but it happens)!

I want to be your confidant; I have unyielding compassion for you and the patience to stick with you through any circumstance. I'll be your best friend and forever responsive to your needs. The unspoken caveat is that I want appreciation and love in return. I want you to like and value me, yet I struggle to believe why you would like me unless I do nice things for you. So, I take care of your needs so that you'll share your love and appreciation with me.

I've spent my whole life keeping my eyes open for people in need and then filling that need—because we both get our needs met that way. But if you ask me what I want or need, I'm baffled. So mine is an awful double bind; I don't know what I need, and if I did, I wouldn't ask for help for fear of losing the people most important to me.

I've learned that flattery earns me a **connection** with others, so I'm constantly scanning for opportunities to affirm and compliment, which means boundaries tend to get messy. I'll do just about anything to gain your approval and become indispensable—hence, it's hard to remain objective when I want others to depend on me. Also, I can get angry when I'm not appreciated; I make your life easier and deserve love and attention in return.

HOW I WANT YOU TO PERCEIVE ME

Helpful, friendly, unselfish, attentive, likable, trustworthy, empathic, valuable, caring, responsive, insightful, indispensable, and valuable.

MY COACHING STYLE

Coaching is my calling! Well, anything where I get to help people is my calling. I innately connect with and help others. I feel confident in my warmth and empathy, and in the coaching profession—serving others gives me purpose.

I can talk all day without getting tired, so I always have energy for everyone. I want to learn about your needs and areas of pain and offer comfort or just be there with you. I'm emotionally robust and can be with my clients in any story they tell. I'm also really good at reading what my client needs me to be, and I can become it.

I've got a positive outlook and quickly see others' strengths. Empowering others is one of my strengths! I enjoy supporting my clients in reaching their goals and witnessing their successes, and it feels good knowing I help people become their best selves and feel good about themselves. It's vital that my clients know I'm invested in their wellbeing, and to make that happen, I go the extra mile to ensure their care. For example, I'll give my clients my cell phone number so they can reach me any time, day or night.

One of my challenges is honoring the direction my clients choose for themselves. Sometimes it's so obvious they'd be happier and avoid missteps if they try things my way. I also don't like it when they're stuck in the mud of negative feelings when I see a clear path out of it, and they don't take it. I can be pretty forceful (in a loving way) when I want them to see the positive things I see in them or their situation.

Another of my challenges is wanting to be everything to every client. I want to know it all and be it all. Sometimes exclusively—I want to be the invaluable support system in their life. Additionally, when clients don't recognize all I do for them, I feel unappreciated and sometimes jealous. I would do anything for them, and I need them to acknowledge my benevolence and appreciate me in return.

WHAT I AVOID

Feeling unappreciated or disliked sends me reeling. If a client says they want to find another coach, I'm sunk—I can't bear the thought of disconnection—actual panic sets in if there's a real fear of losing a client. I do so much for my clients; I need them to acknowledge and value my care and demonstrate their appreciation by maintaining our relationship. I get triggered when I feel a client pull away from me, which is dangerous territory because I may go into overdrive to meet their needs or get angry if I feel rejected.

POSITIVE OUTLOOK

People whose dominant bias is **Connection** shift distressing experiences by aiding others—their positive outlook strategy is affirming you and helping you with your problems. For stability, folks whose dominant bias is **Connection** rely on creating and maintaining relationships. Consequently, to feel panic, distress, or shame signals lost contact, requiring immediate action for reconnection. To reunify the bond and restore love, fulfilling others' needs reframes their distress and offers a solution to the panic of separation and the shame of feeling unworthy.

HOW THIS MIGHT SHOW UP IN COACHING

Without self-awareness, coaches whose dominant bias is Connection may strive to solve client problems to become valued and irreplaceable. Additionally, an over-focus on the positive and frequent compliments may feel Pollyannaish and inauthentic to a client. Needing adoration and appreciation may erase objectivity, empathy, and appropriate boundaries. Also, the care offered may not be benevolent; rather than letting the client find the resources within themselves, being overly helpful meets the needs of those who have a dominant bias toward Connection.

A SCENARIO

Your client tells you that their child died, and they want to see a grief counselor. They don't feel coaching will help them right now, and for financial reasons, they want to stop coaching until further notice. An urgency rises within you to save this relationship. Two issues might emerge, sympathy and a compulsion to keep this client. In desperation, you tell your client that losing another connection at this time may be detrimental to their healing. You remind them of the forward movement they've made with you and how coaching can complement counseling. Your client feels uncomfortable and is not dissuaded and firmly states that this is your last session. In this final moment, you're angry that the client seems to devalue your care and is severing ties to seek other help.

BREATHING PRACTICE FOR DOMINANT BIAS CONNECTION

Breathing is the fastest and most reliable way to return to presence, and particular dominant biases benefit from specific breathing practices. The following breathing practice is adapted from the work of Russ Hudson and Jessica Dibb in their program, *The Enneagram in Conscious Living*.

First, find a comfortable yet alert position in which to sit. Next, bring your attention to the front of your head, the place between and a bit above your eyebrows. You might know it as your 'third eye.' Rest your hands on your lap, palms up or down, whichever feels comfortable. As you inhale softly through your nostrils, keep your attention focused on the location of your third eye—it might help to place a finger there, bringing energetic attention to the area. Then slowly move your focus to the center of your head, smack-dab in the middle of your skull, and momentarily pause as you complete the inhale. Then, as you exhale, imagine your breath slowly leaving from the crown of your head. Remember James Redfield's maxim, "where attention goes, energy flows," and keep visualizing your breath entering, filling, and leaving your Head Center.

Repeat breathing into your Head Center when you notice the urge to help someone or feel unlovable or unloved.

Do this as a daily practice to:

- Access immediate grounding when activated.
- Begin acknowledging and honoring your needs.
- Realize your inherent value and suppressed hostility.
- Develop neural pathways to conscious presence.

Uncover what makes relationships meaningful to you and explore the role of others in your life. Connecting is a strength of yours, but you must arrive without an agenda and with a tangible sense of the coach/client boundary. Finally, recognize that you give to receive and may use affirmation more liberally than needed.

A DEEPENING AWARENESS INQUIRY FOR DOMINANT BIAS CONNECTION

What if **you** are love?

DOMINANT BIAS: GRATIFICATION, DIAGRAM NUMBER: 7

I'm all about adventure and fun! I find pleasure just about anywhere and love spontaneity. I see endless possibilities everywhere, and my positivity helps others feel hopeful. I'm enthusiastic about new experiences, and I can do almost anything I try; luck seems to be on my side. I like taking risks and love taking my friends on adventures they wouldn't usually take, like climbing abandoned buildings and hiking through unknown woods. People seem to feel safe when they're around my positivity and confidence.

I love exploring! Everything is worth exploring: food, people, nature, cities, books— basically anything novel. And I'm a quick study! Sometimes I'm a bit of a know-it-all, but that's just because I'm passionate about everything and learn quickly. Though I admit I have a hard time sticking with something that turns out to be boring—it's not a problem, however, because I've always got something else to do.

I enjoy making people laugh, and I've got a fantastic sense of humor. I want everyone around me to get along because bad juju is rubbish—so I've become great at bringing people together to talk things out when they're squabbling; I'm an extraordinary mediator.

One of my unspoken rules is that the people I care about must be safe; I have many hidden anxieties about my loved ones. Additionally, deep down, there's an emptiness I can't seem to fill, which is why I continually generate excitement and adventure. I don't cope well with pain of any kind and actively avoid my concealed loneliness. My avoidance strategy is finding anything interesting to take me and my thoughts elsewhere quickly.

Despite persistent worry about my loved ones and my habit of avoiding pain, people with broken hearts and sad tales tend to draw me in. I want to listen to their heartache and be the person who can pull them out of it. If there's an underdog, I'll find them and hold them under my wing until they're ready to fly again. I have a natural ability to see the positive potential in everyone and everything, which often seems to support others who are struggling.

I love taking the opposing side in a conversation! Some might call me a mischief-maker. Ha! I am adept at finding a reason to believe the opposite side of an argument, and I'm interested in other points of view. I love an excellent debate! Sometimes my opinions are unpopular, and I like that about myself. It keeps me free to explore options and possibilities (a quality of a stellar coach).

HOW I WANT YOU TO PERCEIVE ME

Fun, adventurous, optimistic, intelligent, busy, needed, charming, generous, fast-paced, spontaneous, witty, happy, and enthusiastic.

MY COACHING STYLE

As I said earlier, I'm a great mediator, and I enjoy differing points of view without judgment, simply curiosity. I genuinely care about people's wellbeing and can hear sad stories and angst. I'm rather curious about people because we're all so different. More clients mean more variety! And because I'm fantastic at recognizing others' potential, I encourage my clients to reframe their experiences in a new, hopeful light.

I have a lot of energy to share with my clients, and because I love learning, I've got a lot of coach training, which makes me versatile. Experiential coaching offers variety and helps me connect with my clients when they are open to it. I've found group coaching exciting because there are many opportunities for fascinating topics, spontaneity, and brainstorming! And more clients mean more potential to use my coaching skills.

However, it's challenging to stay focused when I get bored, and sometimes I find myself mindlessly drifting away. Sometimes, I think about things my clients can do to fix their problems, and sometimes I daydream about my next client or what I want to do when my workday ends. Additionally, I occasionally catch myself offering suggestions rather than encouraging my clients to find their own answers, only because I'm excited about an idea that I know will work.

WHAT I AVOID

I don't often get triggered, but I'll quickly shift the topic to something positive if I am. My biggest problem is getting distracted or so absorbed in my client's stories that I'm not hearing them objectively. Sometimes, if I get bored or the client stays in the same unhappy place, telling me the same depressing story repeatedly, I may get terse. Chronic negativity sucks out all of my positive energy and holds me hostage. Or maybe a client shares a story of such despair that it's just too painful to hear, then I might disappear into my thoughts and daydreams. I think and have often said, "there's no point thinking about this [negative experience] anymore; let's move on."

POSITIVE OUTLOOK

Fearing and avoiding pain is the objective of folks whose dominant bias is **Gratification**. Arising fear alerts them that something needs their attention and quick action. However, those with Gratification as their dominant bias can't handle the pressure of fear and insecurity, so they shift their attention to something exciting or uplifting; they put on a happy face, find some friends, and go on an adventure. Folks who resonate with Gratification often attempt to prove that despite a problem, they're fine. They might tell you, "nothing positive comes out of feeling bad," and turn away even in the most emotionally painful experiences. Instead, they may shift their attention to something fun or reframe their experience as an opportunity.

HOW THIS MIGHT SHOW UP IN COACHING

Without awareness, people whose dominant bias is Gratification will avoid pain and sadness, specifically emotional distress, making it potentially difficult to connect on an empathic level. Preferring positive experiences and emotions, a coach who resonates with Gratification may avoid discomfort and neglect their client's suffering by redirecting painful feelings. Additionally, a coach whose dominant bias is Gratification might try cheering up a client rather than allowing them to feel their distress and sorrow. Finally, when finding themselves somewhere other than a joyful environment, they may escape to their minds and devise a plan for something more exciting.

A SCENARIO

Your client often has dramatic stories and reasons for not working on their goal. For example, today, your client shared that they haven't split up from their partner because their partner needs them. Your client has worked on this goal for five weeks, and every week your client tells you the same story; whenever they try having a break-up conversation, their partner either begins to cry or screams at them to get out. Your client doesn't think they can withstand their partner's sadness or rejection, so they either hug and give in to staying together or beg their partner to let them stay. And beneath all of this, your client complains about feeling trapped and unappreciated.

Finally, you're at your wit's end with no progress on your client's part, and you have no patience to hear the sob story again. You begin to fidget, trying to stay focused, but you're frustrated. You zone out while your client drones on about the highlights and lowlights of their partner, and you begin to wonder if you can continue working with them. While you want to be helpful, you're not going to get stuck in the quicksand with your client.

BREATHING PRACTICE FOR DOMINANT BIAS GRATIFICATION

Breathing is the fastest and most reliable way to return to presence, and particular dominant biases benefit from specific breathing practices. The following breathing practice is adapted from the work of Russ Hudson and Jessica Dibb in their program, *The Enneagram in Conscious Living*.

First, find a comfortable yet alert position in which to sit. Next, bring your attention to the center of your chest. Place both hands in your lap, palms up, or one hand over your heart and the other on your lap, palm up. As you inhale slowly through your nostrils, keep your attention focused on your chest cavity and fill it with air, feeling your ribcage expand. Hold your breath in for a moment and exhale softly through your nostrils, holding out the exhale for an extra pause before taking your next inhale. Alternatively, with both hands over your heart, you might imagine hugging a loved one on the inhale, holding them tight for the pause, and sensing their embrace on the exhale. Remember James Redfield's maxim, "where attention goes, energy flows," and keep visualizing your breath entering, filling, and leaving your Heart Center.

Repeat breathing through your nostrils and into your heart's container when you notice boredom, emotional discomfort, or fear.

Do this as a daily practice to:

- Access immediate grounding when activated.
- Feel safe and grounded.
- Heal your repressed sadness and regret.

• Develop neural pathways to conscious presence.

Practice the skill of pausing. Painful emotions and conversations may trigger fear, anxiety, or boredom. Be aware of your tendency to imagine exciting possibilities and plans as a mental escape. Using your breathing practice, you'll learn to quiet your mind and stay present when discomfort or boredom arises—your client needs to know you're always present and in the room with them.

A DEEPENING AWARENESS INQUIRY FOR DOMINANT BIAS GRATIFICATION

How would *you* be different if you savored every flawless moment in its entirety?

LIVING WITH GRIEF: DAY 90, YOU'RE NOT HERE

We celebrated your birthday on Saturday.

And you weren't here.

We went to Brasa. Like last year.

We sat at the family table like last year.

We reminisced about where you and grandpa Bob sat last year.

We had a meal that would make you proud.

You and I spent your birthday together last year.

You got your first "legal" tattoo.

The one that matches mine.

You were so proud of it that you couldn't keep it covered.

You had to show everyone, especially grandpa, at dinner.

You should be home now. School finished for the year.

But you're not here.

I stare at your picture, and for a moment, you're here.

Just for a moment.

Then I remember you're not here, and you won't ever be here again.

Not in your large, noisy, messy, smiling, busy, know-it-all, physical way.

It can't be true.

Right?

I'm still waiting to wake up.

I'm still waiting for you to come home.

IN CLOSING

The people who resonate with the Positive Outlook Harmonic Group can be an amusing, comforting, uplifting, motivating, and optimistic bunch of folks. However, avoiding painful feelings by distracting themselves and others with comfort, caretaking, anticipation, humor, and denial – while providing pleasurable experiences for others – keeps them from experiencing the full range of emotions and disrupts their ability to address needs appropriately, both theirs and others.

CLOSING INQUIRIES

Coaches can't support another's feelings unless they dare to address their own. Hence, if you recognize yourself in the Positive Outlook Harmonic Group, it's time to hold up the mirror to what you're concealing from yourself. Starting a daily presence practice is ideal if you don't already have one.

Lastly, in your coaching sessions, remember to stay consciously present, keep your inner witness near, remain curious and without an agenda, and coach the person rather than getting preoccupied with their story.

- Do any of the Positive Outlook narratives sound familiar to you?
- What do these descriptions mean to you, even if you don't see yourself in them?
- How will you use this information going forward?

"Anyone who is going through deep grief can tell you that grief affects your mind, your heart, and your body. Having our pain seen and seeing the pain in others is a wonderful medicine for our body and soul."

— David Kessler, *Finding Meaning*

CHAPTER SIX

THE RATIONAL COMPETENCY HARMONIC GROUP

"Yes, one grief unleashes another and another, and having torn open the wound left by the loss of Maude, his mind turned to the most painful loss of all, and the tears ran more abundantly down his face."

— Diane Setterfield, *Once Upon A River*

THE RATIONAL COMPETENCY HARMONIC GROUP

DIAGRAM NUMBERS 3, 1, 5

Chapter 5 explored the Positive Outlook Harmonic Group. Remember that these folks inspire others and lift morale through affirmation, encouragement, optimism, and providing comfort. However, they have an imbalance when addressing needs and unpleasant emotions, both theirs and others. As a result, when feeling uneasy, the people who resonate with one of the Positive Outlook biases tend to distract with redirection, humor, withdrawal, caretaking, aloofness, denial, and escapism.

Now we'll look at the Rational Competency Harmonic Group.

The folks whose *dominant bias* resides in this Harmonic Group stay objective when the pressure is on. They attempt to avoid adversity by keeping feelings at bay and operating efficiently, expertly, and professionally to right what's wrong and fix what's broken. But regrettably, they can create interpersonal strife with an overfocus on rules, structures, and agreements, minimizing or dismissing feelings, judging others as immature or illogical, and may seem pretentious at times. While each point has a unique predilection, those dominant in one of the Practical Competency biases have a shared goal to resolve problems, disagreements, and conflicts sensibly and proficiently.

PAUSE AND REFLECT:

Observe how these dominant biases resonate with you as you read through these three descriptions. Do you see yourself in any of these descriptions? Can you relate to any of these dominant biases? This inner witnessing is the beginning of your exploration.

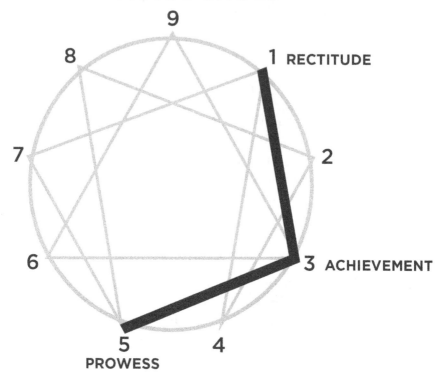

RATIONAL COMPETENCY HARMONIC GROUP

DOMINANT BIAS: ACHIEVEMENT, DIAGRAM NUMBER: 3

I value **achievement** and hard work and strive for recognition for work well done. I aspire to success through ceaseless efforts and will not stop until I've become the greatest at what I do. I am highly goal-oriented and crave appraisal for my achievements; without a doubt, there's no purpose in putting energy into anything that doesn't bring praise and recognition. To that end, I will work tirelessly to meet the grandest of standards.

I know that anything is possible with hard work, and I enjoy empowering others with my confidence and drive. I'm in tune with what society and culture define as successful, and I work to achieve that pinnacle. Average is unacceptable; outstanding and noteworthy is my expectation.

I'm a master people reader and can become what the people around me want me to be. Inspiring others with my accomplishments and triumphs is one of my gifts. Because I thrive on goals, I'm dynamic and focused. I comfortably focus on and champion others and their success, yet I also want to shine as your mentor beneath the surface.

I'm often impatient when blocked from completing a task or goal completion. I don't have time for idle chit-chat like relationship troubles or what you did on the weekend—we're here to work. Having said that, if conversing about what's important to you gets me to my goal, I will do so.

Although I am thorough and efficient, I'll take a shortcut to get to the final product if there's an expeditious way. I love taking hard workers with me as I climb the success ladder, especially if you endorse my excellence, but take heed; I'll leave you in the dust for the chance to shine.

Anything less than outstanding is a failure. I'll do whatever it takes to come out on top, and if I don't, it is not because of a deficiency or error on my part. It's vital to my self-esteem, actually, my entire identity, that you view me as effortlessly flawless. And here's a tip from me: leave the emotions behind—they're mere stumbling blocks to reaching the top.

HOW I WANT YOU TO PERCEIVE ME

Successful, outstanding, dynamic, efficient, focused, driven, talented, exemplar, competent, connected, direct, and confident.

MY COACHING STYLE

I'm all about goals, so coaching feels natural to me. However, sometimes it's difficult to see that I may urge goal setting rather than hearing my client's readiness to create them. Impatience is my Achilles heel, for when I know what my client needs to do but they're not doing it, or when emotions deter their progress, I get mighty frustrated. Be that as it may, I love supporting others' achievements and wish to impart my passion, lighting a fire beneath their efforts. I want to see people become the best version of themselves possible and enjoy championing my clients' achievements.

I move fast, and I appreciate clients who get things done efficiently and without fuss. I'm pretty direct, which is off-putting to some, but again, there's no sense saying or doing any more than is necessary to reach a goal. Two sinkholes I avoid are emotional topics and exploring deep feelings. Though I understand people are complicated, I'm uncomfortable with the messiness of emotions—they merely delay success.

Another snare that traps me when I'm not self-aware is the need to appear competent and praise-worthy. Being astute at reading and becoming what the person I'm with wants to see and experience so that I receive my client's approval and validation can be an underlying need. And though it feels good at the moment, my clients and I can spend a lot of time complimenting each other on our attractiveness, expensive and trendy clothing, luxury cars, extravagant income, status, or a gorgeous new partner.

WHAT I AVOID

I avoid obstacles, failure, and invisibility. Not receiving attention and recognition or hearing others' emotions may trigger my defense system to get down to business (rational competency). Though I'm not aware of it, I get activated when impeded from achieving what will bring me admiration and attention. When that happens, I dominate the situation to regain control, which might mean making impossible demands, stampeding others' feelings, becoming obsessive about efficiency, impatient, competitive, and pretentious.

PRACTICAL COMPETENCE

People whose dominant bias is **Achievement** set aside emotions in service of being remarkable. When pushed, their panic button sends them into high gear to find an efficient solution. Concealing shame and distress is the driver of maintaining their dazzling exterior. But, ultimately, the person from whom they're hiding is themselves—fearing that they are useless, ineffective, and valueless lurks beneath their drive for success.

HOW THIS MIGHT SHOW UP IN COACHING

Without self-awareness and to avoid feelings, coaches whose dominant bias is Achievement may disconnect from their emotions and set to getting things done, eliminating empathy and patience from the coaching equation.

Additionally, a primary focus for those with whom Achievement resonates is others' perception of them. Consequently, addressing and meeting a client's needs is nearly impossible when one's objective is intuiting and becoming what the client wants them to be. Above all, people with the dominant bias of Achievement need admiration and recognition, which can only come from outside of themselves, so their client may become a means to an end for validation and the avoidance of shame and distress.

A SCENARIO

As soon as the conversation begins, your client starts talking about their ex. Once again, they want to discuss what might be keeping their ex-partner from committing to their relationship. Digging into the psyche of your client's ex is not how you want to spend this session; it's unproductive, repetitive, and irritating. While your client seems unable to get past this loss, you're not prepared to talk about it again. You remind your client that thinking about an old relationship is getting in the way of their forward movement, and ask them if they're ready to talk about their goals.

BREATHING PRACTICE FOR DOMINANT BIAS ACHIEVEMENT

Breathing is the fastest and most reliable way to return to presence, and particular dominant biases benefit from specific breathing practices. The following breathing practice is adapted from the work of Russ Hudson and Jessica Dibb in their program, *The Enneagram in Conscious Living*.

First, find a comfortable yet alert position in which to sit. Next, bring your attention to the center of your chest. Place both hands in your lap, palms up, or one hand over your heart and the other on your lap, palm up. As you inhale slowly through your nostrils, keep your attention focused on your chest cavity and fill it with air, feeling your ribcage expand. Hold your breath in for a moment and exhale softly through your nostrils, holding out the exhale for an extra pause before taking your next inhale. Alternatively, with both hands over your heart, you might imagine hugging a loved one on the inhale, holding them tight for the pause, and sensing their embrace on the exhale. Remember James Redfield's maxim, "where attention goes, energy flows," and keep visualizing your breath entering, filling, and leaving your Heart Center.

Repeat breathing through your nostrils and into your heart's container when you detect an over-focus on productivity, achievement, or the denial of your emotions.

Do this as a daily practice to:

- Access immediate grounding when activated.
- Recognize your need for others' validation.
- Heal your shame and realize your innate value.
- Develop neural pathways to conscious presence.

Observe your internal shift that initiates action—what emotions lie beneath your flurry of activity? Practice recognizing and identifying your concealed feelings. Notice your tendency to see life as a series of goals and the safety net these goals provide. Stop *doing* and ask yourself what's igniting the need for recognition and validation.

A DEEPENING AWARENESS INQUIRY FOR DOMINANT BIAS ACHIEVEMENT

Who are **you**, if not your achievements?

DOMINANT BIAS: RECTITUDE, DIAGRAM NUMBER: 1

I desire integrity, balance, and order; my radar looks for what needs improving. I am hard-working, responsible, and often perfectionistic. You can count on me to follow the rules and strive for everyone, including myself, to be fair, just, and virtuous while endeavoring for a balanced, harmonious world.

I've got a loud inner critic telling me what I'm doing wrong and highlighting what others do wrong. So it's nearly impossible to see what's going well for me and others because there's always something needing refinement. My motives, however, are for us all to feel aligned with everything good and pure.

To avoid criticism and blame, I adhere to high standards. If accused or attacked, I'll push back because I don't need reminding of the plethora of flaws I possess. I worry that my defects make me unlovable and work fastidiously to stay in your good graces. Conversely, my self-evaluating lens turns outward, judging and evaluating those around me, which doesn't earn me fans.

Worry and constant inner dialogue are part of the package with me because there's so much that needs modifying, correcting, or fixing. However, if you tell me that my worrying is needless, I'm likely to say, "It's not worrying; it's looking at alternatives that could make things better."

I value precision, and when communicating, I'm direct and articulate, and I expect the same from you. As a career, I make an excellent judiciary or engineer because evaluation and discernment are two of my strengths. The trouble is that people might experience me as scolding, rigid, obsessive, and irritable. But please don't forget that I'm also competent, calm, rational, sensible, and willing to improve.

HOW I WANT YOU TO PERCEIVE ME

Polite, self-contained, fastidious, organized, responsible, proper, capable, courteous, prompt, accurate, and blameless.

MY COACHING STYLE

I'm astute at noticing where development is needed; my coaching style is to find practical ways to resolve what's wrong, incomplete, disorganized, or shoddy. I appreciate order and restoring it in times of need, and I love helping others improve themselves. However, self-improvement and the improvement of others can become another fix-it project for me. And while I'm supportive of others' emotional challenges, I tend to keep my tender feelings sealed off, which is a boundary that can become a barrier.

I feel most purposeful with forwarding movement in whatever task is in front of me and inviting others to feel the satisfaction of a job well done. Sometimes, however, we humans are complicated, and I feel impatient when others don't do their part. Now and again, my patience runs thin, but I don't give up; somehow, I'll find a way to repair what's broken.

It can be difficult to admit there are other ways of doing things, including coaching. So while I'm interested in different methodologies, I can be rigid in my coaching approach, which means I may be limiting my capabilities and my client's potential.

WHAT I AVOID

I avoid being wrong, bad, and making mistakes. I want to be accurate, pristine, and void of fault, though I know it's futile because we're all flawed. When I make a mistake or do something wrong, my habit is tensing up and feeling anxious and worried about the consequences. I get irritated when others don't follow the rules or do the right thing and often remind others when they don't do what's right. I obsess over my mistakes, often avoiding anticipated persecution with self-reproach and contrition. Lastly, I avoid carelessness and imperfection by tending to things myself, which breeds resentment; I often say, "If you want something done right, you have to do it yourself."

PRACTICAL COMPETENCE

Internally, folks whose dominant bias is **Rectitude** assess anger and rage as bad or wrong and, for that reason, restrain both of these emotions. Sensibly inhibiting their anger and rage, these folks choose to focus on what needs doing, and whatever it is, they do it with precision. Likewise, those who resonate with Rectitude tend to see the world as broken and intend to fix it with a keen eye for noticing flaws. Accordingly, irritation and frustration often replace the unacceptable emotions of anger and rage and fuel the energy needed to right what's wrong.

HOW THIS MIGHT SHOW UP IN COACHING

Coaching draws folks whose dominant bias is Rectitude, both clients and coaches. There's an opportunity for self and other development with coaching; however, being messy, imperfect creatures, humans resist change and resent judgment which can cause interpersonal dissonance in a coaching relationship. The high standards of folks who resonate with Rectitude may infect a coaching relationship with expectations. Mirror neurons allow humans to share and understand emotion. Yet, those with this dominant bias tend to repress emotions, diminishing their empathic capacity and ability to create a safe space for vulnerability.

A SCENARIO

Your client tells you that their youngest son enlisted in the army, and he'll leave in three weeks. While in boot camp, the recruits can't communicate with anyone outside of their base except by snail mail. Your client is experiencing loss and emotionally preparing for and agonizing about severing ties with her son. Still, because you understand the logic behind the army's rule, you tell your client that the no-contact regulation of boot camp is a standard that's been around since its inception. You explain to your client that it's in place to rewire the recruit's brain by severing familial ties so that they are emotionally unaffected at times of war and can take action without stopping to think or feel. While this might be true, logistics are not helpful; your client needs empathy and acknowledgment of their feelings, not facts.

BREATHING PRACTICE FOR DOMINANT BIAS RECTITUDE

Breathing is the fastest and most reliable way to return to presence, and particular dominant biases benefit from specific breathing practices. The following breathing practice is adapted from the work of Russ Hudson and Jessica Dibb in their program, *The Enneagram in Conscious Living*.

First, find a comfortable yet alert position in which to sit. Next, bring your attention to the front of your head, the place between and a bit above your eyebrows. You might know it as your' third eye.' Rest your hands on your lap, palms up or down, whichever feels comfortable. As you inhale softly through your nostrils, keep your attention focused on the location of your third eye—it might help to place a finger there, bringing energetic attention to the area. Then slowly move your focus to the center of your head, smack-dab in the middle of your skull, and momentarily pause as you complete the inhale. Then, as you exhale, imagine your breath slowly leaving from the crown of your head. Remember James Redfield's maxim, "where attention goes, energy flows," and keep visualizing your breath entering, filling, and leaving your Head Center.

Repeat breathing into your Head Center when you feel irritated or frustrated or notice an urge to improve, fix or correct someone or something.

Do this as a daily practice to:

- Access immediate grounding when activated.
- Recognize the repressed resentment and tension carried in your body.
- Begin healing your perceived imperfections.
- Develop neural pathways to conscious presence.

Noticing the physical tension that arises when triggered is your cue to re-route impending irritation. Instead, invite presence by allowing discomfort and flaws. Thinking you've done something wrong causes worry, anxiety, and probably the urge to defend your position or explain your actions—signifying you've energetically left the conversation. Practice feeling uncomfortable, allowing deficiencies and foibles to exist in yourself and others, rather than reacting to them with reproach or reformation.

A DEEPENING AWARENESS INQUIRY FOR DOMINANT BIAS RECTITUDE

Who are **you** with everything in its place and nothing to improve or fix?

DOMINANT BIAS: PROWESS, DIAGRAM NUMBER: 5

I value knowledge as the gateway to surviving life on earth. But I have some insecurity about knowing enough to live this human life. Sometimes, I feel paralyzed by the struggle to figure things out, and then I miss out on actively living what I'm learning. So, I retreat and continue absorbing information instead of putting knowledge into action.

My learning style is not merely acquiring what scholars and books tell me; I prefer to master the topic of interest. At times, the plethora of wisdom in the world can immobilize my decision-making ability. Yet, deep down, I fear inadequacy and inferiority and feverishly learn to prove my worth to myself and others.

Unfortunately, I habitually isolate myself while gathering information, making it hard to connect with people. Be that as it may, the world expects a lot from me and frequently usurps my energy. For that reason, I prefer autonomy and immensely enjoy observing, researching, and absorbing information. Furthermore, the more I know about a subject, the more confident and secure I feel. Therefore, I don't ask much of others and appreciate a solitary existence. Not that I avoid people, I'm merely aware of my energy reserves and portion appropriately—if I don't ask much of others, others won't ask much of me.

I love knowledgeable conversation; it's what ignites my fire. However, don't ask me to talk about emotions, or it'll be a short conversation. I prefer to live in a small domicile without fanfare and can be protective of the few objects I own. Additionally, I'm prone to hoarding my energy and feelings.

When I'm present, I have direct contact with knowledge and awareness. By that, I mean it's not what I read in books or online that illuminates what I'm trying to grasp, but the answers to what I'm searching for wondrously appear in my mind. I guess it's kind of like intuition or gnosis. It's clarity for facts or truth that arrives without effort—but only when I'm present.

HOW I WANT YOU TO PERCEIVE ME

Knowledgeable, competent, innovative, private, autonomous, curious, inquisitive, capable, and discerning.

MY COACHING STYLE

I'm pragmatic and interested in facts rather than feelings, which can be a blindspot for my coaching. When I stay curious about humans and what makes them tick, I have an easier time connecting with and staying focused on my clients and their experiences.

Some people experience me as prosaic because removing my 'expert hat' is counter-intuitive. While I want to share my expertise with others, I have difficulty balancing analysis and emotion and can sometimes seem pompous. I'm proficient with Motivational Interviewing; asking questions is easy. Additionally, recognizing the stage of change in which my clients reside comes easily. However, my practicality and usual lack of affect can be off-putting when compassion is required.

Desiring mastery makes it challenging to enter into a partnership such as coaching. Being an authority keeps me safe, and saying "I don't know" often feels fatal. However, remembering that coaching is about curiosity and collaboration rather than expertise helps me stay grounded and present.

WHAT I AVOID

Feeling unprepared, incapable, or intellectually deficient brings insecurity, which causes withdrawal and the urge to study and master the intimidating topic while recharging my energetic battery. Likewise, when I feel backed into a corner, overwhelmed or depleted, I emotionally detach and retreat from everyone and everything, including myself, to return to stasis.

PRACTICAL COMPETENCE

Folks whose dominant bias is **Prowess** prefer privacy, so when they experience fear or anxiety, they welcome the opportunity to reinforce what's most comfortable; solitude. Securing safety within their minds, they amass their most precious resource—intellect. Advantageously, people who resonate with Prowess have a habit of solitary research and analysis which may create uncertainty or doubt in potential antagonists, providing an additional energetic and physical safeguard.

HOW THIS MIGHT SHOW UP IN COACHING

Folks whose dominant bias is Prowess tend to avoid emotion and become energetically drained when engaging with others. So, with feelings and engagement as cornerstones of coaching, empathy, and the energy to stay present may prove challenging without self-awareness. Additionally, hiding in their preferred comfort zone, the Head Center, a coach who resonates with Prowess, may inadvertently create an interpersonal emotional void. Moreover, favoring the expert role makes coaching counter-intuitive and may lead to advice-giving, and any perception of superiority sensed by a client will surely hinder connection.

A SCENARIO

Your client, a mother of a one-year-old, tells you that she's decided it's time to stop breastfeeding. You think this seems reasonable since the child is a year old. However, you didn't count on your client spending your session sobbing about severing the mother/child bond and fearing the decision is cruel. After all, the baby isn't rejecting breastfeeding; your client decided that a year of breastfeeding is sufficient. But now that it's here, she feels cruel and selfish and wonders if their bond will change. You have never breastfed a child and have no second-hand experience with it, so you're perplexed about an appropriate response. You sense a surplus of emotions you don't understand and have no time to research.

Feeling uncomfortable, you pretend to know more about this topic than you do. You explain that the secession of breastfeeding is a natural transition and that your client's child cannot breastfeed forever. You remind her that she's fortunate to have had the last year bonding with her infant in this way. From what little you know, you tell her about the health benefits she's provided her baby this past year. And you remind her that she's not losing her baby; she's gaining freedom.

You've successfully responded with practicality when your client needed emotional mirroring, demonstrating the potential emotional void created by Practical Competence.

BREATHING PRACTICE FOR DOMINANT BIAS PROWESS

Breathing is the fastest and most reliable way to return to presence, and particular dominant biases benefit from specific breathing practices. The following breathing practice is adapted from the work of Russ Hudson and Jessica Dibb in their program, *The Enneagram in Conscious Living*.

First, find a comfortable yet alert position in which to sit (you may also do this breathing practice while standing). Then, with your eyes open in a gentle gaze, bring your attention to your belly. Keep both hands on your lap, palms down, or one hand on your stomach, laying your other hand palm down in your lap. Breathe deeply through your nostrils, allowing first your stomach and then your rib cage to expand. Hold your breath in for a moment before exhaling slowly through your nostrils. Feel the relaxation of your chest, rib cage, and belly. Take a brief pause before beginning your next inhale. Remember James Redfield's maxim, "where attention goes, energy flows," and keep visualizing your breath as a wave that travels down to your Belly Center and then up, expanding and raising your chest cavity.

Repeat this breathing exercise when you notice yourself escaping to your mind and retreating from the world.

Do this as a daily practice to:

- Access immediate grounding when activated.
- Heal repressed feelings of rejection and futility.
- Assuage the urge to hoard your time and energy.
- Develop neural pathways to conscious presence.

Learn to recognize the urge to retreat from interaction and people. Practice the breathing technique above to identify the emotion(s) causing your reactivity so that you can detect it in a coaching session. Practice the skill of pausing and returning to conscious presence with an assurance that there is no threat to your personal resources. Coaching appointments are time-bound, always allowing for energy replenishment.

A DEEPENING AWARENESS INQUIRY FOR DOMINANT BIAS PROWESS

How will you be changed when you know that *you* are the source of ceaseless joy?

LIVING WITH GRIEF, DAY 119, THE FUTURE

Yesterday the future was dark.

There was nothing there when I looked.

No color. No people. No earth.

I dreamt of you, Nicholas, last week. You told me matter-of-factly that you couldn't come home. I pleaded for you to come back.

I told you it didn't matter what you had done or what you wanted to do with your future. Just please come home.

You said you could not.

I dreamt of you, Dad, last week. You told me matter-of-factly that you wanted to prepare me for your departure.

I turned away from you. I began to cry and didn't want you to see. But, then, you told me again that I needed to prepare because you would be leaving.

I remained turned away, sobbing.

My dreams this week are of Joey dying. In the dream, I don't know how he dies; I am merely living in the aftermath of his death.

Dad, you were there last night, too. We were in the dining room at 2017.

I was trying to create terrariums. I was very focused. It was imperative to complete them.

I looked at you, and you watched me collapse and scream and beat the floor because Joey was dead.

I went to other places in the dream and tried not to think about Joey's death. And then I would, and again I would collapse and weep and beat the floor.

Today the future looks like an endless, winding sidewalk with nothing and no one on either side. And for every section I traverse, just one square at a time, I know I will break down and fall into my pain and weep.

IN CLOSING

With the Rational Competency Harmonic Group, you can always count on things getting done efficiently, professionally, and effectively. However, focusing on rules, agreements, and structures while accomplishing tasks, completing projects, and solving problems means denying or diminishing emotions, keeping others at bay, and decreasing life's full range of experiences and emotions.

PAUSE AND REFLECT:

Develop a project to meet and greet the full range of your emotions!

CLOSING INQUIRIES

Coaches can't support another's feelings unless they dare to address their own. Hence, if you recognize yourself in the Rational Competency Harmonic Group, it's time to hold up the mirror to what you're concealing from yourself. Starting a daily presence practice is ideal if you don't already have one.

Lastly, in your coaching sessions, remember to stay consciously present, keep your inner witness near, remain curious and without an agenda, and coach the person rather than getting preoccupied with their story.

- Do any of the Rational Competency narratives sound familiar to you?
- What do these descriptions mean to you?
- How will you use this information going forward?

"The mightiest power of death is not that it can make people die, but that it can make the people left behind want to stop living."

— Fredrik Backman, *My Grandmother Asked Me to Tell You She's Sorry*

CHAPTER SEVEN

THE EMOTIONAL REALNESS
HARMONIC GROUP

"For me, my grief is like a huge hole. Everything flows around that hole. I have forced myself to move forward, but I can never move on."

— Lisa See, *The Tea Girl of Hummingbird Lane*

THE EMOTIONAL REALNESS HARMONIC GROUP

DIAGRAM NUMBERS 6, 4, 8

Chapter 5 explored the Positive Outlook Harmonic Group and its dominant biases. The folks who resonate with Positive Outlook inspire others by focusing on the positive. However, they also have an imbalance in addressing needs and unpleasant emotions, both theirs and others. As a result, they can overdo affirmations and encouragement to avoid painful feelings and relational discord and view others as too negative.

Chapter 6 explored the Rational Competency Harmonic Group and its dominant biases. These folks operate efficiently, professionally, and expertly when a problem needs solving or in times of duress. However, they also minimize or dismiss feelings, theirs and others, while overfocusing on rules, agreements, and structures and can sometimes appear arrogant.

Now in Chapter 7, we delve into the Emotional Realness Harmonic Group.

Without hesitation, the folks whose dominant bias resides in the Emotional Realness Harmonic Group tell you when they have concerns, experience difficulties, or feel dissatisfied. Their often direct and sincere reaction to unmet needs can sometimes be intimidating or immature, creating more interpersonal trouble than the initial offense. However, they may view others as insensitive or dishonest while seeking assurance that the other person is similarly authentic in feeling and perception of the current issue. Those who resonate with Emotional Realness are masters of mirroring emotional authenticity and providing a safe space and an invitation for any emotion or topic.

PAUSE AND REFLECT:

Observe how these dominant biases resonate with you as you read through these three descriptions. Do you see yourself in any of these descriptions? Can you relate to any of these dominant biases? This inner witnessing is the beginning of your exploration.

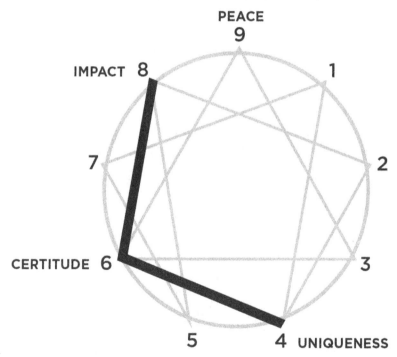

EMOTIONAL REALNESS
HARMONIC GROUP

DOMINANT BIAS: CERTITUDE, DIAGRAM NUMBER: 6

I am someone you can count on—my loyalty is unwavering. I'm structured, dependable, and empathic about life's stressors. I'm adept at looking at situations from all sides, really digging into what might be the best route forward. I love supporting people as they create and work toward what's most meaningful for themselves. Support and trust are vital in my relationships, and I'm excellent at creating a safe space and nourishing trust.

I welcome any topic and can sit with you in whatever's getting in your way or hurting you. I'm curious and have a great imagination; brainstorming ideas is one of my strengths. I love searching for possibilities to support what's important to you, and I believe in you and your ability to achieve everything you want. Safety is vital, and I'm on the lookout for possible threats—we'll work together to keep you safe.

Another of my strengths is curiosity, and I love testing the limits of a theory. However, it needs to stand up to my scrutiny to believe in something. People and things have to withstand my appraisal to prove their value, and if I don't feel secure around you, I'll back away.

I tend to be pessimistic and prone to inflating what might go wrong. And I'm inclined to "analysis paralysis;" I'll research until there's nothing left to learn about a subject and ask the opinions of my closest friends, and still find it hard to make a final decision—because I might make the wrong decision!

I'm a planner, which eases my worry and anxiety. Routine and structure are my friends. However, I've learned that one must still have a plan B, C, and maybe even D in case of an emergency. I'm often stuck in indecision or take impulsive action to quiet my mind—though neither seems to work. My mind never stops looking for the best course of action and avoiding disaster. And yet I have a hard time trusting that I can make the right decision. I guess that's called indecision.

On the high side, I find clarity and inner knowledge about what's right when I'm present. I can stay attuned and attentive to what's right in front of me rather than the countless potential disasters. Being present is when I feel at my best—it's when I feel grounded.

A bit of advice from me: it's good practice to carry a Swiss Army Knife and a first-aid kit at all times. And just in case, keep an emergency kit in your car (with scheduled inspection of its contents and replacing what's expired). You never know when you or someone else might need help.

HOW I WANT YOU TO PERCEIVE ME

Loyal, prudent, capable, inquisitive, reliable, dependable, engaging, adherent, supportive, interested, and structured.

MY COACHING STYLE

I'm attentive, curious, and empathic with my clients. I want to understand what makes my clients tick to serve them best. I create a safe and trustworthy environment and pledge my commitment to them. I'm unafraid of big emotions and relish supporting my clients through painful experiences. Meaningful conversations build bonds that last a lifetime. Through thick and thin, I am a steady resource.

I'm deeply interested and invested in those I care about, including my clients. It's an honor to use my knowledge to empower my clients to achieve their goals. I'm a fantastic problem-solver and pay close attention to what my clients say. I have an inner sense of what is most helpful for my clients, though sometimes I second-guess myself. I'm humble and enjoy giving my clients the chance to shine. Teamwork is a vital ingredient in all aspects of my life.

I trust that each client knows what they need. I believe everyone has a sense of purpose, and I enjoy helping others explore theirs. I'm fully invested in my client's welfare and will faithfully work on their behalf.

WHAT I AVOID

Feeling betrayed, threatened, or backed into a corner will raise my hackles. Hopefully, those things won't often happen within my professional relationships. I feel anxious when I don't have an answer or when I'm unprepared, and when that happens, I can lose my footing and begin over-thinking. From there, I self-doubt, which leads to worry and angst about making the right decision and feeling safe again. Practical tasks help me refocus sometimes, but that isn't always feasible, for instance, when I'm with a client.

EMOTIONAL REALNESS

Experiencing a certain level of fear is part of the deal with **Certitude** as a dominant bias. As with everyone, the activation of fear happens when the psychological needs of security, safety, and stability go unmet. Fear's activation reinforces its prominence and the resulting hypervigilance, emotional intensity, or withdrawal (physical or mental) depending on the offending person or situation. In hopes that someone will step in with guidance and protection, the folks who resonate with the dominant bias **Certitude** can be emotionally boisterous. If a loud, emotional expression isn't possible for some reason, disappearing (metaphorically or physically) may restore safety and stability.

HOW THIS MIGHT SHOW UP IN COACHING

Without self-awareness, a coach whose dominant bias is Certitude may struggle with boundaries as they want to be strong and capable, yet guidance from others offers assurance. Because feeling secure in their relationships is essential to folks who resonate with Certitude, dependency on and appeasement from their clients is an area to watch. Additionally, fear may sever presence or become defensive (emotional realness) if this coach feels insecure about their coaching skills and safety or doubts their client's loyalty.

A SCENARIO

After reminding you of their horrible marriage, your client tells you they're finally getting divorced. Understandably, anger dominates their recount of the past week. Your client thanks you for everything you've done for them and tells you they're moving back to Florida, where the rest of their family resides. Assuming you're losing a client, doubt about your coaching skills, abandonment, and feelings of confusion and betrayal sneak into your thoughts. Insecurity and worry keep you from offering telephonic coaching with this client, and you're pissed off that they put you in this position. With this distressing information, what's erupted is the urgency to protect yourself, making presence and connection impossible.

BREATHING PRACTICE FOR DOMINANT BIAS CERTITUDE

Breathing is the fastest and most reliable way to return to presence, and particular dominant biases benefit from specific breathing practices. The following breathing practice is adapted from the work of Russ Hudson and Jessica Dibb in their program, *The Enneagram in Conscious Living*.

First, find a comfortable yet alert position in which to sit. Next, bring your attention to the front of your head, the place between and a bit above your eyebrows. You might know it as your' third eye.' Rest your hands on your lap, palms up or down, whichever feels comfortable. As you inhale softly through your nostrils, keep your attention focused on the location of your third eye—it might help to place a finger there, bringing energetic attention to the area. Then slowly move your focus to the center of your head, smack-dab in the middle of your skull, and momentarily pause as you complete the inhale. Then, as you exhale, imagine your breath slowly leaving from the crown of your head. Remember James Redfield's maxim, "where attention goes, energy flows," and keep visualizing your breath entering, filling, and leaving your Head Center.

Repeat breathing into your Head Center any time you notice worry or doubt about your ability to make sound decisions.

Do this as a daily practice to:

- Access immediate grounding when activated.
- Recognize and acknowledge your fear.
- Begin healing your anxiety and self-doubt.
- Develop neural pathways to conscious presence.

Practice recognizing your emotional activation by asking yourself, "Where is my attention?" You're not with your client when you're over-thinking, even if it's on your client's behalf. Being in just this present moment is the safest and quickest way to soothe your mind. Breathe into your Head Center until you sense the peacefulness of not thinking; then, you will access clarity and knowing without effort and angst.

A DEEPENING AWARENESS INQUIRY FOR DOMINANT BIAS CERTITUDE

What if **you** are the valuable resource guiding and living your life?

DOMINANT BIAS: UNIQUENESS, DIAGRAM NUMBER: 4

I see beauty everywhere—the world is full of cohabiting, nuanced darkness and light. I know I am a remarkable gift to humanity, and though misunderstood, I accept the world may not be ready for my particular sensitivity. I'm not afraid of suffering; I see it as a gateway to authenticity and welcome the opportunity to delve deeply into yours.

People seem content with our culture's superficial nature, chasing after unnecessary objects and people to validate their worth and happiness. But I know they're not happy; they merely live in a film designed by humanity. Yet, remarkably, a part of me longs for the simplicity of "fitting in with the Joneses." Oh, to have the splendor of emotional ignorance. But, alas, I don't understand that world, and it doesn't understand me.

Often marred by hurt and shame, my past defines my present. Still, I am courageous enough to sit with you in your suffering because of my early wounds. I long to feel the sorrow and delight of others, and empathy comes naturally, making me an inherently earnest coach.

I want you to know the depth of me and appreciate my singularity. I bring receptivity and imagination to our abused world, drawing out the vibrant colors, flavors, smells, and tastes. Yet, I feel melancholic about the cruelty set upon our earth and all of its inhabitants.

I describe my world through poetry, music, and the arts—they lend a depth of expression found nowhere else and allow for mystery, depth, and intimacy. And likewise, I must surround myself with someone who exemplifies who I am, which can be onerous because I'm emotionally complex and want to stay that way.

I have a habit of comparing myself to others, which means I spend a lot of time evaluating myself and others, thus contributing to my shame. I notice individuality and weigh others against my version of unique and special, which often leads to envy. I want to be mysterious, yet I sometimes resent being misunderstood. Sadly, I sense that I don't fit in anywhere and can spend considerable time in self-pity.

HOW I WANT YOU TO PERCEIVE ME

Expressive, authentic, memorable, sensitive, unique, empathic, creative, inspired, magical, appealing, grand, and valuable.

MY COACHING STYLE

I enjoy getting deep and dirty with feelings. I'm unafraid of complex emotions and encourage you to let loose whatever needs releasing. I believe we're all unique, and I see your individuality. I can match your pace and savor whatever feelings arise. I recognize what's beautiful and share what I see with you.

I look in your eyes and feel your past wounds. And with interest, I hear your stories. Moving forward from painful feelings may be difficult, yet I believe that you will become your courageous and authentic self. I want to be with you as you escape the discomfort that brought you to coaching and stand with you while you explore the future.

I want you to feel accepted for who you are and feel safe in my presence. I have so much to offer you! Humans are tortured beings; let's stand together with open hearts and heal our suffering.

WHAT I AVOID

I avoid the mundane and trivial and being average or predictable. Feeling misunderstood triggers me, yet I know I'm mystical and esoteric. Superficial topics bore me and are unbefitting. So if others aren't willing to be authentic and courageous with their feelings, I won't stick around. Furthermore, I avoid people and places that don't validate my creativity and beauty.

EMOTIONAL REALNESS

Feeling invisible, unimportant, or misunderstood ignites distress and shame for those who resonate with the dominant bias of **Uniqueness**. They experience their emotions intensely and yearn to share them with others. Resonating with Uniqueness, these individuals long for emotional mirroring yet expressively resent the implication of sameness. Authenticity and deep conversation are vital, and global issues such as climate change, war, and violence can drown them in sorrow. Emotional Realness is a cornerstone for those who resonate with Uniqueness, as acting in service of their feelings is essential in all areas of life.

HOW THIS MIGHT SHOW UP IN COACHING

People with a dominant bias toward Uniqueness are comfortable with complicated feelings and excel at empathy. However, without self-awareness, their intensity may overwhelm a client. Additionally, a client's emotional withdrawal may elicit panic in a coach who resonates with Uniqueness. Further, objectivity may be difficult if this coach identifies with their client's feelings, and longing for emotional rescue may create countertransference. Lastly, comparison and judgment feed individuality, negatively impacting objectivity, empathy and creating a safe environment.

A SCENARIO

Your client shares that they've never felt comfortable in their body, and after many conversations with their partner, they've decided to begin a gender reassignment process. First, however, they tell you that they want to continue coaching through the entire process to stay focused on their treatments and responsibilities.

You nearly cry at the massive vulnerability they've shared with you. Instantly, you feel a kinship, an immense bond. Of course, you will continue as their coach; you tell your client you feel honored to be a part of their care team. You want to learn more about their decision and begin gently probing, but your client shows signs of discomfort. You can't understand why; they've just shared a vital truth.

Your client tells you they don't want to talk about the details, reasons, or feelings about the procedure; they merely want to be held accountable for their obligations. You don't understand their secrecy and feel slighted. You sense an invisible barrier has just erupted between you, and you recede slightly.

Feeling insecure and excluded, you begin to protect your wounded heart. Focusing only on tasks when a significant physical and emotional transformation is at stake feels inconceivable.

BREATHING PRACTICE FOR DOMINANT BIAS UNIQUENESS

Breathing is the fastest and most reliable way to return to presence, and particular dominant biases benefit from specific breathing practices. The following breathing practice is adapted from the work of Russ Hudson and Jessica Dibb in their program, *The Enneagram in Conscious Living*.

First, find a comfortable yet alert position in which to sit (you may also do this breathing practice while standing). Then, with your eyes open in a gentle gaze, bring your attention to your belly. Keep both hands on your lap, palms down, or one hand on your stomach, laying your other hand palm down in your lap. Breathe deeply through your nostrils, allowing first your stomach and then your rib cage to expand. Hold your breath in for a moment before exhaling slowly through your nostrils. Feel the relaxation of your chest, rib cage, and belly. Take a brief pause before beginning your next inhale. Remember James Redfield's maxim, "where attention goes, energy flows," and keep visualizing your breath as a wave that travels down to your Belly Center and then up, expanding and raising your chest cavity.

Repeat this breathing exercise when you notice longing, envy, or feelings of rejection.

Do this as a daily practice to:

- Access immediate grounding when activated.
- Heal your negative self-image and that of others.
- Begin emotionally supporting yourself.
- Develop neural pathways to conscious presence.

Emotional reactivity may impede authentic connection with your client and is your cue to pause and use the breathing technique you've practiced to reclaim objectivity. Change your physical position while breathing into your belly until you notice your activation lessen—you might even get up and walk around if you're able. Then, when you're selflessly able to mirror your client again, you're ready to rejoin the conversation.

A DEEPENING AWARENESS INQUIRY FOR DOMINANT BIAS UNIQUENESS

Discovering that you are the love for which you long, who are **you**?

DOMINANT BIAS: IMPACT, DIAGRAM NUMBER: 8

I am a person of action. I find enjoyment in having a sense of purpose and indulging in its cause: business, child-rearing, friendships, athletic activities, or the Enneagram. I dream big and get to work making my dreams happen. I don't always plan my route, but I make wise short-term decisions that later pay off.

I'm intensely protective of those I love, especially *my* people. I've got a filter that scans for what's unjust in the world, and if I find a transgression, someone will hear about it. When I commit to something or someone, it's 150%. However, proving your worth comes before receiving that level of commitment from me. Likewise, you'll likely never hear from me again if you betray or try to control me. I'm forthright and demand the same from others; no beating around the bush or messing about with passive-aggressive bullshit, please.

I have a sensitive side, but few people see or experience it. I won't complain when I'm hurt, physically, emotionally, or mentally. However, you might know something's amiss because anger becomes more frequent. I will force and fight to overcome and endure the things that immobilize others, and I have the strength and courage to hold you and your pain when you need support.

Power and I engage in a persistent and unrestrained dance. I strive to be powerful and independent, and I derive great pleasure from empowering others. I will do anything to raise the oppressed, but I won't carry anyone forever; you've got to stand on your own two feet and self-advocate. You have to demonstrate that you're not weak or dependent, or I'll walk away.

I'll admit, patience is not one of my strong suits—I wanted action and results yesterday! Nevertheless, I believe in humanity's magnificence and relish finding another's strengths, raising them to be their best selves (when they're willing to do the hard work, of course).

People often tell me I'm too direct and can be overbearing, intimidating, and sometimes even aggressive. And it's true; I like to have things my way—if I'm in charge, no one can take advantage of me. Indeed, avoiding vulnerability means keeping the emotional gates shut, sometimes leading to seclusion. Accordingly, I sense myself as an island needing perpetual defending from predators.

One thing is for sure; I will go up against the mightiest and most threatening opponents in support of myself and those I love. My fear of vulnerability extends far beyond me to my loved ones. Subsequently, the ruination of my loved ones is far more terrifying than my own demise.

HOW I WANT YOU TO PERCEIVE ME

Assertive, independent, confident, driven, direct, impervious, honorable, controlled, decisive, protective, fearless, responsible, and strong.

MY COACHING STYLE

I am honored that you are my client and promise to give everything I have to support your development. I look forward to intense discussions about leveraging your strengths to move you toward your vision. I will support you when you feel emotionally wounded and empower you to overcome challenges. Whatever skills I possess are yours; let's fill your toolbox together!

I see possibilities you may initially overlook, and I love witnessing your tenacity to stretch your emotional comfort zone. I excel at envisioning what needs deconstructing and reconstructing to bring your vision to life. Whether learning to say 'no' or cleaning out your closet (literally or figuratively), I see the big picture and break it into bite-size chunks with you.

I'm direct and will illuminate what you don't or can't see. And though I'm excited to get you moving, I do my best to use my coaching skills to ask questions so that you find the answers in your time. It's much more rewarding seeing your "Ah-Ha" moment than it is to tell you the contents of your roadblock. You can also count on me to be dependable, responsive, and authentic, and I welcome every emotion you bring to our conversations!

WHAT I AVOID

It's a brief yet thorough list: weakness, cowardice, undependability, self-righteousness, arrogance, and inauthenticity. Maybe that's not so brief? If I sense any of these things, I will usually challenge you or withdraw my effort—I'm not going to invest if you aren't on the up and up. And I'm not here to blow sunshine up your ass—I'm here to work hard and expect the same from you. In our coaching relationship, I hold us both accountable for showing up and giving 100% effort, investment, courage, respect, common sense, curiosity, and humility. Likewise, I feel confident we can move mountains together if we do these things.

EMOTIONAL REALNESS

Fearlessly and clamorously sharing their anger and rage is a given for folks whose dominant bias is **Impact**. Anger is a comfortable emotion, and those who resonate with Impact readily react to its emergence. Their survival instinct is to be robust and fearless, thus triumphantly overpowering rivals. As a result, they believe they are invincible and are unafraid to express their anger and rage. However, softer emotions and vulnerability are another story.

HOW THIS MIGHT SHOW UP IN COACHING

Loyalty and justice are vital to those who resonate with the dominant bias of Impact. Without self-awareness, feeling challenged or betrayed may cause a defensive response, perhaps frightening a client and destroying trust and security in the process. Further, not recognizing their physical manifestations of anger and the immediacy of reaction may damage the safe space necessary for coaching. For those who resonate with Impact, habitually avoiding vulnerability and over-focusing on strength cheats their clients of the essential mirroring needed to experience their vulnerability. Finally, over-protecting a vulnerable client might blur professional boundaries, leading to a power differential similar to a parent/child relationship rather than a partnership.

A SCENARIO

Your client tells you they've just learned they're pre-diabetic and hypertensive. They hate themselves for letting themselves go and gaining weight and decide they're ready to focus on getting their health back; it's been too long since they felt good. You're three weeks into sessions surrounding weight loss and sugar elimination and reviewing their goals. For the third week in a row, and after modifying and reducing the difficulty of the goals each week, your client continues to eat donuts, frappuccinos, fast food, and ice cream daily.

You're frustrated that they come back week after week without trying. You'll support change but resent wasting your time on someone who doesn't want to change. You confront your client on their behavior by asking why they continue to show up for coaching without doing any work outside of your conversations. And putting the ball in their court, you tell them that unless they're going to follow through with their action plan, there's no sense in scheduling future appointments.

BREATHING PRACTICE FOR DOMINANT BIAS IMPACT

Breathing is the fastest and most reliable way to return to presence, and particular dominant biases benefit from specific breathing practices. The following breathing practice is adapted from the work of Russ Hudson and Jessica Dibb in their program, *The Enneagram in Conscious Living*.

First, find a comfortable yet alert position in which to sit. Next, bring your attention to the center of your chest. Place both hands in your lap, palms up, or one hand over your heart and the other on your lap, palm up. As you inhale slowly through your nostrils, keep your attention focused on your chest cavity and fill it with air, feeling your ribcage expand. Hold your breath in for a moment and exhale softly through your nostrils, holding out the exhale for an extra pause before taking your next inhale. Alternatively, with both hands over your heart, you might imagine hugging a loved one on the inhale, holding them tight for the pause, and sensing their embrace on the exhale. Remember James Redfield's maxim, "where attention goes, energy flows," and keep visualizing your breath entering, filling, and leaving your Heart Center.

Repeat breathing through your nostrils and into your heart's container when you notice your emotions rising for a discharge or an urgency to control a situation.

Do this as a daily practice to:

- Access immediate grounding when activated.
- Soften your emotional reactivity.
- Find strength in vulnerability.
- Develop neural pathways to conscious presence.

Reactivity comes fast for those who resonate with the dominant bias **Impact**—making their point known feels urgent. Learning the physical activation cues creates an opportunity for objective responding rather than subjective reacting. It will take commitment to a daily grounding practice to trust the safety and impact of not reacting. Practice grounding and pausing every day—it won't be easy, so remember that power and strength include stillness, silence, and vulnerability.

A DEEPENING AWARENESS INQUIRY FOR DOMINANT BIAS IMPACT

Who are *you* without perpetual intensity and struggle?

LIVING WITH GRIEF: DAY 148, STILL HERE

Grief. When does it ease?

After Nicholas died, I remember my therapist telling me that my grief would be different in five months. Was there something more to what she said? I can't remember.

His death was traumatic and shocking nearly five months ago.

So what about now? What's onboard after five months? Pain. Despair.

Do you know how long life sounds when despair is forever?

Some people think I'm doing okay. Some people tell me how strong I am. Some people say I'm resilient.

They don't know me.

They don't know the loss of a child.

They are not watching their other children suffer.

The guilt and worry parents carry become lethal when their child dies tragically.

People are full of worries that don't matter. I was one of them.

So many regrets. So much self-loathing. So many if only's and what if's.

I wish I had dared to pay attention to what mattered when I had the time. I regret spending my emotional energy on people and things that took me away from my children.

IN CLOSING

There's no shortage of emotion for the folks who resonate with the Emotional Realness Harmonic Group. Emotions often feel urgent and authentic, making them hard to contain. Others might find their emotional reactivity threatening or scary, activating the other person's defense strategy, thus escalating the dialogue. However, their authentic emotions also create a welcoming environment to explore a full range of feelings.

A WRAP-UP AND THE HARMONIC GROUPS' TRUE MAGIC

Initiating the resolution of disagreements, conflicts, or those moments when we might try to avoid an uncomfortable topic (like grief, trauma, and loss) are where the Harmonic Groups shine. First, however, is recognizing where your pattern lies, which is why we've spent three chapters helping you uncover your Harmonic Group pattern. Once you know yours, step two is doing your best to identify the Harmonic Group strategy of the other person with conscious presence.

It's not usually difficult to notice if someone is Emotionally Real, practicing Rational Competence by problem-solving, or attempting to evade discomfort with some form of Positive Outlook. So, armed with your best guess in mind, validate the other using their Harmonic Group strategy and then introduce the best version of yours. So, for example, if you happen to utilize Rational Competency and your client's pattern falls in the Positive Outlook Harmonic Group, and a triggering topic just arose, you might say, "I notice you using your strength of positive reframing, Client. What doors does that strength open for you?"

To take it one step further, after recognizing your Harmonic Group strategy, in this case, Emotional Realness, and that of the other, Rational Competency this time, invite the Harmonic Group strategy not present in your conversation (Positive Outlook). It might sound like, "I see you getting right down to business to find a solution, Client. What's the opportunity here if you include emotion in the equation?"

If you suspect your Harmonic Group strategies are the same, you might wonder how to proceed. In that case, it's vital to bring in at least one other Harmonic Group strategy, preferably both. For example, let's pretend you both have dominant biases in the Positive Outlook Harmonic Group, and your client shares something disquieting. Here, depending on your flavor of Positive Outlook, you might be inclined to redirect the conversation while your client minimizes its impact with laughter. In this example, leveraging both Emotional Realness and Rational Competency, you might ask, "What emotional impact does this experience have on your future, Client?"

CLOSING INQUIRIES

Coaches can't support another's feelings unless they dare to address their own. Hence, if you recognize yourself in the Emotional Realness Harmonic Group, it's time to hold up the mirror to what you're concealing from yourself. Starting a daily presence practice is ideal if you don't already have one.

Lastly, in your coaching sessions, remember to stay consciously present, keep your inner witness near, remain curious and without an agenda, and coach the person rather than getting preoccupied with their story.

- Do any of the Emotional Realness narratives sound familiar to you?
- What do these descriptions mean to you?
- How will you use this information going forward?

"Each of us needs periods in which our minds can focus inwardly. Solitude is an essential experience for the mind to organize its own processes and create an internal state of resonance. In such a state, the self is able to alter its constraints by directly reducing the input from interactions with others."

— Daniel J. Siegel, *The Developing Mind: How Relationships and the Brain Interact to Shape Who We Are*

PART 3

PUTTING IT INTO ACTION

CHAPTER EIGHT

GETTING PRACTICAL

"She's looked into the books her dad reads about "mental coaching," and they talk about the brain having to steer the body but that sometimes the reverse is the only way to survive. She's seen depressed adults do the same thing: keep moving, exercising, and cleaning and renovating their summer cottages, finding things that force them to get up in the morning: plants to be watered, errands to be run, anything, so they don't have time to think about how they feel. As if we hope that physical activity, tiny everyday rituals, might lull the anxiety to sleep."

— Fredrik Backman, *Us Against You*

BEING SKILLS

We're going to explore some coaching conversations in a moment, incorporating what you learned in earlier chapters. But first, I'd like to touch on some particulars of *coaching presence* and the coaching conversation.

THE BASICS

Hopefully, your coach training included the following skills, which are helpful to fall back on when addressing an unfamiliar or uncomfortable topic rather than offering socially patterned affirmations.

- Coach approach, not expert approach
- Client leads conversation
- Inquiries with no preset conclusion
- Comfort with silence
- Listening to the person, not the story
- Succinct client-centered reflections and affirmations
- Asking permission when appropriate
- Curiosity *without* a need to know
- An absence of agenda, attachments, or need to perform
- Exploring; not offering solutions, or fixing
- Presence and empathy

WHAT'S NEXT

As we've explored at length, you must know your triggers to access your coaching skills in an uncomfortable conversation rather than relying on social norms. So thank you for taking the time to read this book; I appreciate that you want to do more for your clients than repeating the platitudes they hear from everyone else.

CONSIDER THIS:

I've included the Enneagram in this book as an opportunity for you to widen and deepen your recognition and understanding of your triggers, patterns, strengths, and blind spots. This book is in no way exhaustive; indeed, you are just scratching the Enneagram's surface with what I've included here. Learning and practice are lifelong endeavors. Even the most knowledgeable and experienced teachers don't feign expertise. You'll find an appendix at the end of the book with my best suggestions for further study.

As you peruse the guidance and scenarios in this and the following chapter, I invite you to leave space for noticing how your reactions might provide hints about your Enneagram dominant bias. Understanding your personality and instinctive patterns is only as helpful as the time you spend paying attention.

When learning about the Enneagram, it's easy and exciting to feel like an instant expert and hold tight to whichever personality you decide sounds most like you. Still, I encourage you to keep an open mind because often, where we first land is where we'd like to be, not where we are.

Additionally, please avoid using the information in this book to "type" others, especially your clients. It's fun and natural to want to understand others, but the Enneagram requires a long personal tenure before earning the ability to help others explore their type. Finally, no person or online test can tell anyone their Enneagram dominant bias; each individual must find that independently.

THE GENERAL OUTLINE

While there is no easy coaching response for grief, trauma, and loss, there are some guidelines for when you're engaging in difficult conversations with your clients. Below is a conversation outline that might be useful. However, as a reminder, to be calm and available when a client throws you a heavy topic, you must engage in consistent breathing practice, like those in the three previous chapters, so that your mind and body know what to do when faced with these difficult conversations and topics. Imagine if a runner didn't train for their 100-mile trail run yet arrived on race day, trusting their current fitness level would see them through!

Being Skills

I. Practice listening for experiences of loss and trauma.

- As we've explored, loss includes more than death, and your client *may* need help exploring the emotional impact of their loss or trauma.

- To help you identify loss, remember that it is *struggling against the reality of one's current circumstance and missing what used to be.*

II. With your inner witness, recognize your physical manifestations of distress as they're happening—they might give you a hint that an emotionally charged topic is afoot.

- Do your hands get clammy?
- Does your heart race?
- Does your breathing change?
- Do you have a tightening in your abdomen?
- Maybe you notice your legs want to get you out of there?
- Do your shoulders begin to ache?
- Do you feel suddenly tired?
- Do you get a headache?
- Perhaps you find yourself distracted from the conversation?
- Something else?

III. Self-regulate when necessary using your presencing skills.

- Remember, you must have the ability to return to objectivity or risk providing less than your best coaching. Practice your breathing exercises daily so you can center yourself at any moment.

- Use the information in the previous chapters about your potential Enneagram dominant bias for self-regulation, presence, and breathing practice.

IV. Objectively refocus on your client when triggered.

- Once re-centered, energetically sense and listen to your client (not their story). Again, quoting Isabel Wilkerson, "listen with a humble heart to understand another's experience from their perspective."
- Utilize the Harmonic Groups and Enneagram dominant bias material to bolster your ability to refocus.

V. Be with your client, don't *do coaching to* them.

- Be authentic and intentional while holding (not owning) your client's experience.
- Do away with your plan, don't try to perform, say the right thing, or be impressive.
- Be a witness—your client needs your courage, patience, compassion, radical empathy, and unstated hope.

THE COURAGE TO STAY PRESENT

Clients actively try to cope with their ethereal reality and loss by talking about it and comprehending what may be incomprehensible. In essence, it is significant when your client tells their story and reveals the source of their grief to you. If their experience is fresh, they may repeatedly tell their story, so stay present and follow their timeline, not yours.

Sometimes, a client's recalled experience may be emotionally triggering for you. However, there's an opportunity in these moments to build rapport and authentic mirroring when you stay consciously present.

CONSIDER THIS:

You may well be in your client's shoes one day if their loss is a parent or caregiver. Always respond thoughtfully and specifically to the client you're with rather than offering a convenient or hasty adage—as you'll also appreciate it someday. Rather than saying, "I can't imagine what you're going through," consider one's need for *relatedness* and conceptualize what they are going through from their perspective and respond from that place.

There is no "right thing" to say, but know that leaning on trite phrases creates distance between you and your client. Your client senses your escape from their discomfort when you echo platitudes. Moreover, like trying to find the right thing to say, if you think about how your empathy is extraordinary or that you're an empath in these moments of client vulnerability, you are not with the griever; you're lounging in self-flattery. So, instead, be courageous, envision their pain, and respond without attachment. To do otherwise is a disservice to your client.

When our clients suffer, they want certainty where this is little. To create a safe and solid coaching environment, we're responsible for self-regulating our emotions. Again, this is where knowing your Enneagram dominant bias and inner witness is invaluable, as both elucidate your habitual emotional patterns.

Discomfort may fill the space between and around you and your client, yet you must be the one stable thing in the room, allowing your client's pain a place to land. Clients need the compassion, hope, and time that witnessing provides while seeking their new reality's foundation.

PAUSE AND REFLECT:

Empathic inquiry is not probing but inviting; we might mirror our client's experiences and emotions by sharing observations and asking thoughtful questions. Empathic questions are not, "Oh my gosh, are you okay?" Or, "How are you managing?" Instead, it might be, "What would it mean to you to feel a sense of stability, Client?

COMPETENCE

With great love comes great suffering. That includes all of the losses discussed in this book—a loved-one, safety, traditions, and humanity, to name a few. In whatever we invest ourselves, our energy, and our time, if it's lost, the grief is immense. A hard pill to swallow at times, but there's no getting around pain if we choose to live and love.

Respecting the client's pace and grieving method is essential because the suffering caused by loss and trauma is unexpected, uninvited, and does not follow a predictable path. We reinforce our client's *autonomy* and *competence* when our clients steer the conversation and when we remember that coaching is their time and agenda, not ours. Accordingly, bring curious innocence to your sessions to learn something from each grieving client rather than imposing a plan.

CONSIDER THIS:

Don't expect expediency from grief. If your client needs to weave stories of their suffering into each session for two years, so be it. You won't always need to respond to it, but don't discount grief by forcing topics about the sunny side of life or suggesting ways to move on. Conversely, if your client never talks about their suffering or the experience that delivered it, it does not mean they are cured, recovered, fixed, reformed, mended, or "back to normal."

PAUSE AND REFLECT:

Though we know that some people are prone to bypassing difficult emotions with positivity or busywork, what looks like emotional avoidance or denial are not issues requiring your intervention. Make no projections or assumptions about your client, their experiences, or their Enneagram dominant bias. Instead, use the Enneagram's wisdom to know and regulate *yourself.*

Remember to stick to the present and future while leaving the past to the counselors and therapists. Yet, of course, if your client might benefit from seeing a counselor or therapist, make the referral.

RELATEDNESS

Your clients may share details about their lost loved ones—welcome whatever they share as part of their process. Remembering our basic need for *relatedness*, one of the most precious gifts you can give your clients grieving the loss of a loved one is asking for their loved one's name. Take care to use the present tense when speaking about your client's loved ones.

If you see a smile on your client's face as they talk about a loved one, ask what's coming up for them. And if there are tears, don't assume you know what they're about; instead, ask, "what are the tears about right now, Client?" One caveat, however, is to make sure that any questions you ask are for your client's benefit and not your curiosity.

CONSIDER THIS:

As you know, some people adeptly name feelings, and others disconnect from them. When your clients are ready to name their emotions, finding gentle ways to help them explore and understand their feelings may help restore their sense of *autonomy* and *competence*. As we all know, emotions can be large, unyielding, and arrive uninvited. Learning to manage them is a long and often unconscious process (not the same as ignoring or overriding them). Listen for the feelings behind the stories and, with compassion, help your clients connect the dots between emotion and language. Remember the value of "name it to frame it."

Additionally, your client may report how busy they are taking care of necessities, buying a headstone, setting appointments, or packing belongings. Indeed, these tasks might restore some sense of *autonomy* and *competence*. However, for you to assume they've moved to the "next stage" of grief and treat them as such is an invalidating mistake. Unbeknownst to your client, they may be in shock, depending on the event's recency and impact. Your job is to create a safe space for your client to **be** while supporting their forward movement.

PAUSE AND REFLECT:

Make no assumptions about your client in a grief process; grief is not linear. Hence, refrain from analyzing or collating what you hear; there is no logic or predictability to grief. Albeit, without a doubt, a stable coaching relationship supports your client's *relatedness* needs, so remember, your client lost something vital, and they need somewhere to secure their emotional footing.

AUTONOMY

Experiencing trauma strips us of certainty and, often, safety, and without these two things, we also lose a sense of *autonomy*. Yet, likely to meet our *relatedness* needs, groups of people sharing a difficult or traumatic experience often find ways to come together, though not always intentionally. By way of example, consider Alcoholics Anonymous or an oncologist's waiting room.

What do you suppose happens when people who share an experience share the same space? The answer: without a need to speak, they mirror hope to one another amid their pain. Together, they are safe from platitudes, advice, pity, and comparison, and they invite vulnerability. It is with protected *autonomy* that they witness one another.

CONSIDER THIS:

Sometimes, a person who experiences trauma or loss also senses a loss of identity. They might feel that somehow, an evaluative invisible sign has appeared across their forehead, announcing their frailty to the world and igniting shame:

"I was raped."

"My child died."

"I'm the only Asian here."

"I have cancer."

"I have an eating disorder."

"I'm infertile."

"My parent beats me."

"My spouse committed suicide."

"My sibling is addicted to drugs."

A sense of separateness and shame arises when we feel different or judged, inviting labels and deprivation of our identity and bringing suffrage to our *relatedness* and *autonomy* needs. Additionally, threats or injuries to our safety and certainty deprive us of competence. Accordingly, an injured perception of identity has dire consequences or all three Centers of Intelligence.

PAUSE AND REFLECT:

Focusing your conversations on your client and not their stories can help them know that they are not at fault, shameful, alone, or in danger; instead, a tragedy has happened to them. Hence, supporting the separation of self from the event helps to alleviate *shame* and insecurity, allowing for healing and hope over time.

This dynamic identity shift demonstrates why it's vital to focus on our clients and not their stories.

SCENARIO

Now that we've laid the groundwork let's run through a scenario that might activate an emotional reaction and explore how to manage your responses to stay present with your clients.

Remember the Being Skills discussed earlier in the chapter and how you might use those strategies to listen, witness, and stay present with clients that might present similar scenarios to those featured here.

CONSIDER THIS:

My intention is for you to feel better prepared and comfortable with emotion regulation, no matter your Enneagram dominant bias, Center of Intelligence, Harmonic Group, or the topic at hand. In addition, I hope to provide a helpful resource for exploring your feelings and reactions when faced with an unfamiliar or emotionally laden coaching topic.

As a reminder:

I. Listen for experiences of loss and trauma.

II. With your inner witness, recognize your physical manifestations of distress as they're happening—they might give you a hint that an emotionally charged topic is afoot.

III. Self-regulate when necessary using your presencing skills.

IV. Objectively refocus on your client when triggered.

V. Be with your client, don't *do coaching to* them.

SCENARIO: ME

I spent Saturday morning running errands for home-improvement projects. While shopping, I purchased peach gummy rings for my son away at college; they're gross if you ask me, but he loves them. I gathered Werther's candies to send along, too; also a favorite of his.

Nicholas and I spoke on the phone the night before; he had a rough morning at school, so we made the time to connect at the end of the day. We talked about Christmas plans and making key lime pie because it was one of his grandpa's favorites (this would be our first Christmas without Grandpa Bob).

Also, during the conversation, Nicholas told me he had decided to complete his internship at home after Christmas rather than go to Wyoming. I was so excited for him to come home at Christmastime that I could barely contain my excitement. But, you know, I tried to play it cool so my enthusiasm wouldn't sway his decision back the other way.

We talked about the show Lost, which Nicholas recommended to me years earlier and then abandoned after I passed the episode he last watched. Always competitive. He thought he might be ready to pick it up again because he knew it was a show about grief. Nicholas hoped it would help him manage his own grief about Grandpa Bob.

Lastly, Nicholas and I made a plan to talk on the phone every Sunday at 10:51 a.m. because that was the precise last time I spoke to my dad, Nicholas' grandpa Bob, not long before having a heart attack on his way to our house for a celebration for Nicholas. My relief and joy were palpable, knowing I would talk to Nicholas in two days and have a standing phone call with him each week.

This emotional and vital conversation excitedly prompted the purchasing of peach gummy rings and Werther's candy for a care package.

Upon returning home from the morning errands, I puttered around the yard, doing what – I can't remember anymore. Then, while walking from the front to the back yard, a police officer met me halfway. My youngest son, not unfamiliar with getting into trouble, prompted my first response; "Oh no, what has Joey done now?" But instead of answering, the officer asked if we could speak inside.

So, of course, I agreed, and we went into the house. He asked if I was Nicholas' mom, and I said yes while remembering a classmate of Nicholas' who had some trouble with the law when Nicholas was home during his last break, just five weeks prior. I immediately assumed there was news regarding the other student. But instead, the police officer went on to say, "The Dutchess County Sheriff's office contacted us. Nicholas died unexpectedly."

The rest is a horror film my mind created to erase the information I just heard. I screamed, over and over, "No!" And at some point, I shouted for Joey to come down from upstairs. However, I couldn't say the words to him; instead, I shoved him in the direction of the police officer while telling him something like, "You go hear for yourself." Then, Joey was standing in front of me while we both looked at the police officer, my partner, standing next to the officer, said to Joey, "Nick is dead."

So much screaming. I remember seeing our neighbor across the street running toward our house, and all I could think was I couldn't entertain or talk to anyone. I yelled, "get him away from the house!" I couldn't understand why the police officer wasn't taking care of this person running up my front steps. Where was the fucking police officer? Instead, Joey ran out the front door screaming at the neighbor to leave.

I still don't know where the police officer was or when he left. My mind imploded; I couldn't think; I had to find Nicholas and straighten this out. But no, I had to call people to tell them. Who the fuck has to call people to tell them their son is dead? I could not make sense of what my mouth needed to say. How does one find the words? Surely, this is not my truth. Surely, Nicholas did not leave me here without him.

PAUSE

TAKE A MOMENT TO CONSIDER WHAT'S ARISING IN YOU

What emotions do you notice?

- Frightened, shocked, or anxious? Agitated, irritated, or numb? Forlorn, sorrowful, or nurturing? Distressed, awkward, or uneasy? Nervous, tense, or confined? Other?

Where in your body do you sense your emotional reaction?

- Is your gut or your mind tied in knots? Clammy hands or physical agitation? A racing heart and increased breath rate? Shoulders and upper back feel tense and tight? Other?

What actions are your feelings prompting you to do?

- Physically or mentally retreat? Talk fast or fall silent? Look away or pace the room? Lean forward? Or an urge to offer a hug?

PAUSE AND REFLECT:

What would you say to a client after hearing this story?

It's easy to get emotionally swept down a familiar neural pathway when a painful or uncomfortable story triggers us. Still, we know that that's not helpful for the client counting on our presence.

What have you learned about yourself with this exploration?

PRESENCE PRACTICE

If you're willing, please try one or more presence practices from the three Harmonic Group chapters (also listed below) before diving into more scenarios in Chapter 9: Coaching Conversations. Feel free to use the one suitable to your suspected dominant bias or all three. Plan to spend five minutes engaging in this practice before moving on.

Remember, this is called a Practice, not a "Do It Right." You're merely following your breath using one or all of these methods, and when you notice your mind going elsewhere, simply bring your attention back to your breath—no need to assign pressure where none is required.

BREATHING PRACTICE FOR THE POSITIVE OUTLOOK HARMONIC GROUP (9, 2, 7)

First, find a comfortable yet alert position in which to sit (you may also do this breathing practice while standing). Then, with your eyes open in a gentle gaze, bring your attention to your belly. Keep both hands on your lap, palms down, or one hand on your stomach, laying your other hand palm down in your lap. Breathe deeply through your nostrils, allowing first your stomach and then your rib cage to expand. Hold your breath in for a moment before exhaling slowly through your nostrils. Feel the relaxation of your chest, rib cage, and belly. Take a brief pause before beginning your next inhale. Remember James Redfield's maxim, "where attention goes, energy flows," and keep visualizing your breath as a wave that travels down to your Belly Center and then up, expanding and raising your chest cavity.

BREATHING PRACTICE FOR THE PRACTICAL COMPETENCY HARMONIC GROUP (3, 1, 5)

First, find a comfortable yet alert position in which to sit. Next, bring your attention to the center of your chest. Place both hands in your lap, palms up, or one hand over your heart and the other on your lap, palm up. As you inhale slowly through your nostrils, keep your attention focused on your chest cavity and fill it with air, feeling your ribcage expand. Hold your breath in for a moment and exhale softly through your nostrils, holding out the exhale for an extra pause before taking your next inhale. Alternatively, with both hands over your heart, you might imagine hugging a loved one on the inhale, holding them tight for the pause, and sensing their embrace on the exhale. Remember James Redfield's maxim, "where attention goes, energy flows," and keep visualizing your breath entering, filling, and leaving your Heart Center.

BREATHING PRACTICE FOR THE EMOTIONALLY REAL HARMONIC GROUP (6, 4, 8)

First, find a comfortable yet alert position in which to sit. Next, bring your attention to the front of your head, the place between and a bit above your eyebrows. You might know it as your 'third eye.' Rest your hands on your lap, palms up or down, whichever feels comfortable. As you inhale softly through your nostrils, keep your attention focused on the location of your third eye—it might help to place a finger there, bringing energetic attention to the area. Then slowly move your focus to the center of your head, smack-dab in the middle of your skull, and momentarily pause as you complete the inhale. Then, as you exhale, imagine your breath slowly leaving from the crown of your head. Remember James Redfield's maxim, "where attention goes, energy flows," and keep visualizing your breath entering, filling, and leaving your Head Center.

Now that you have taken the time to spend five minutes centering, how has it changed your present awareness?

LIVING WITH GRIEF: DAY 159, FLOODING MEMORIES

I've been dreaming about you, but I don't remember the dreams. I only know that you are on my mind when I wake.

I've been thinking about you, specific things we did together, things that made you happy, things like trips to Target.

You knew how I dreaded going to Target, and you loved it. I could count on you to go with me, and I anticipated spending money on something you wanted. Buying something for you was worth your presence.

Trips to the grocery store (Kowalski's) were always a favorite; it was the most fun when we walked. Again, there would be something there you wanted, but it was worth the price of spending time walking there and back with you.

Old Navy for back-to-school clothes; you would pick anything with a Hawaiian print, even if it meant wearing shorts during the winter.

How you loved going out for lunch.

I remember HiLo with Joey, with french fries, glazed donuts, malts, and mac & cheese. You always wanted to try something new, and if it was spicy, all the better.

I remember the French Hen where you took me for my birthday last year. It was so important to you that you paid for my birthday lunch. I had a pancake, and you had something benedict (and critiqued the recipe). I have not been back since.

My first visit to Alma was with you for lunch. I don't know what you were more proud of; me being there or showing me where you worked. Maybe both? We ordered all of your favorites.

I will never forget how your face lit up when I would visit Brasa when you were working. You were so happy to make me whatever special was on the menu and send me home with all my favorites (butterscotch pudding, sweet plantains, and mac & cheese - but only if up to par).

You were the first person to see my newest bike. I rode to Brasa after picking it up. Even when I didn't eat there, you were excited when I stopped by to see you.

I don't know how to express the depth of my gratitude that I could show you my new bike; what a silly thing. But back then, I knew where to find you, and I could see your smile. I remember the visceral butterflies deep in my belly as I rode to see you that day.

I remember how you loved it when I came to your school, for any reason. You lit up when you saw me in the hall or your classroom. From the time you were in kindergarten up until you didn't want to set foot in the high school anymore (because you were better than that) and went off to Metro State, you always looked forward to me being there.

And I remember your frisbee golf field trip! Neither of us knew what we were doing, but we had a lot of fun and laughter trying.

You would love the recent blasts of snow we've had, Nicholas. And you equally would hate the shoveling that goes along with it. Remember when you got mad while shoveling and threw the shovel and stormed off, saying, "This sucks, I'm done!" Patience and exertion were not your strong suit.

I remember you saying "bet."

I guess it was an affirmation, an agreement.

And you called everyone "chef" on your last visit home. A nickname picked up from the CIA.

And then there's "Yeah Squidward." A ridiculous memory for just a few of us that will last forever.

While I cherished the opportunity to see you happy at all of these moments and still do, I wish more than anything that memories aren't all that I have left.

IN CLOSING

Grief is part of the human experience and arrives in our coaching conversations, whether we're comfortable with it or not. Therefore, the coaching elements shared in this chapter point not to specific coaching skills but rather to the coach's *presence* and *being*. If we have sufficient coach training, our conscious presence, not coaching expertise, directly teaches how to be with and what to do with sorrowful and distressing topics.

CLOSING INQUIRIES

You may notice that self-reflection and inner witnessing take considerable attention, especially when new to you. Self-awareness requires much of our attention, but not in the comparative, evaluative way we usually ponder ourselves. Inner witnessing means non-attachment of our observations. Instead, we hold ourselves accountable for our presence.

- On a scale from zero to 100, what percentage of your energy do you allot to staying present in a client's company?

- What do you see changing in your future conversations about grief, loss, and trauma?

- What assumptions do you have about grief, loss, and trauma?

"No matter how they grieve, they share a need for their grief to be witnessed. That doesn't mean needing someone to try to lessen it or reframe it for them. The need is for someone to be fully present to the magnitude of their loss without trying to point out the silver lining."

— David Kessler, *The Sixth Stage of Grief*

CHAPTER NINE

COACHING CONVERSATIONS

"She was asking how to live after a loss like this.
How to pick up one child and let the other go.
How to keep breathing after you whisper, goodbye."

— Kristin Hannah, *The Nightingale*

SCENARIOS

In Chapter 8, we discussed a Being Skills framework for coaches as they practice conscious presence when hearing their client's stories of trauma, grief, and loss. These Being Skills enable you, the coach, to listen, witness, and stay present with clients and their narratives.

So next, we'll explore several examples of actual narratives to see how you might apply what you've learned so far. I've removed or altered any identifiable details, but the stories are genuine. When you've completed this chapter, I hope you feel armed with knowledge and skills to regulate emotionally, no matter the topic.

If you need to take a break or pause to recenter yourself during this segment, please take care of yourself. Of course, because this is not an actual coaching situation, you can control the pace at which you move through this material.

As a side note, one of the advantages of seeing these conversations in print is that the digital coaches out there can also get a sense of how much work they needn't put into their written coaching conversations. Coaches tend to get bogged down in reflecting on everything they hear and digging for details. What our clients need are conscious presence and inquiries that create self-awareness.

As a reminder:

I. Practice listening for experiences of loss and trauma.

II. With your inner witness, recognize your physical manifestations of distress as they're happening—they might give you a hint that an emotionally charged topic is afoot.

III. Self-regulate when necessary using your presencing skills.

IV. Objectively refocus on your client when triggered.

V. Be with your client, don't *do coaching to* them.

Each example includes:

1. Client: The client's presenting topic

- Injured need(s) from a Self-Determination Theory perspective

2. Coach: A typical coach response
   - Plausible Harmonic Group influence

3. Revision: A concise, client-centered response
   - International Coaching Federation (ICF) Coaching Competencies demonstrated

As you read these scenarios and the two responses, notice your internal reactions to each.

EXAMPLE 1: TRAUMATIC LOSS

CLIENT:

"I will be indisposed for a while. My daughter was killed yesterday, and I'm not doing so well."

- Injured need(s): Relatedness, Competence

COACH:

"I'm so, so sorry for your loss, client. Thank you for sharing it with me. I can't imagine what you're going through. Maybe I can help you find a grief counselor."

- Plausible Harmonic Group influence: Rational Competency

REVISION:

"Oh, Client. [Silence to provide space and time for the client to continue.] **What would be most helpful today?"**

- ICF Coaching Competencies: Cultivates Trust and Safety, Maintains Presence, Listens Actively, Embodies a Coaching Mindset

EXAMPLE 2: TRAUMATIC LOSS (CONTINUED)

CLIENT:

"I'm trying, but I don't feel able to even get out of bed today. I picked out her headstone yesterday, and today I have to finish paying for the services. I am overwhelmed and very depressed."

- Injured need(s): Competence, Relatedness

COACH:

"I'm glad you feel safe to share this with me, client. I hope that you know you can share anything here. Have you found a counselor to talk to? I'm sure others out there know exactly what you're going through, maybe a grief group would help. If we were to look for your bright star, what's something positive that gets you out of bed in the morning?"

- Plausible Harmonic Group influence: Positive Outlook

REVISION:

[Silence to provide space and time for the client to continue.]

"With just our call in mind, what would be a helpful outcome today, Client?"

- ICF Coaching Competencies: Listens Actively, Maintains Presence, Establishes and Maintains Agreements, Embodies a Coaching Mindset, Cultivates Trust and Safety

EXAMPLE 3: NEW CANCER DIAGNOSIS

(With an established client and known health history.)

CLIENT:

"Hi, Coach. I have to share. I got my results back, and I do have breast cancer. I must have done something in a past life. Someone is testing me to see how much I can handle. It's just one more thing."

- Injured need(s): Autonomy, Competence

COACH:

"I appreciate that you're telling me about the diagnosis, Client; that's awful news. It really does seem like you've been dealt a hard blow lately. What happens next? How can you take extra care of yourself this weekend, some splurge you might give yourself, like a massage?"

- Plausible Harmonic Group influence: Positive Outlook, Practical Problem Solving

REVISION:

"What makes it important to share this with me today, Client?"

- ICF Coaching Competencies: Maintains Presence, Evokes Awareness, Embodies a Coaching Mindset, Cultivates Trust and Safety, Listens Actively

EXAMPLE 4: NEW CANCER DIAGNOSIS

CLIENT:

"The only place I don't feel out of place or judged is in the oncology waiting room. At least we understand one another there. Most people are afraid of me when they hear I have breast cancer, as though it's leprosy. They back away, which leaves me feeling like even more of a freak than I already am. Who will I be with no breasts?"

- Injured need(s): Relatedness, Competence

COACH:

"Thank you for sharing this with me, Client. It can't be easy living with a diagnosis like cancer. Maybe there's a way to focus on what the cancer's remission will offer rather than what it takes away from you? Are there support groups you can join?"

- Plausible Harmonic Group influence: Practical Competency, Positive Outlook

REVISION:

"Who do you want to be, Client?"

- ICF Coaching Competencies: Evokes Awareness, Listens Actively, Embodies a Coaching Mindset, Cultivates Trust and Safety, Maintains Presence

EXAMPLE 5: TRAUMATIC LOSS

CLIENT:

"My baby sister passed away Wednesday, and we had her memorial today. I have no desire to track [meals] or eat at all. Most days, it's been rather difficult."

- Injured need(s): Relatedness, Competence

COACH:

"Oh, no. I'm sorry for your loss, Client. I can't imagine losing my sister; I don't think I could eat for days after such a loss. How are you taking care of yourself right now?"

- Plausible Harmonic Group influence: Emotional Realness, Rational Competency

REVISION:

[Silence to provide space and time for the client to continue.]

"I noticed an energy shift as you said 'most days, it's been rather difficult.' What are you sensing right now?"

- ICF Coaching Competencies: Evokes Awareness, Maintains Presence, Listens Actively, Embodies a Coaching Mindset, Cultivates Trust and Safety

EXAMPLE 6: TRAUMATIC LOSS

CLIENT:

"Coach, I can't seem to get back on track. All I seem to be able to do is weigh in each morning. I'm doing better and not crying daily about my little sister, but still concerned about my dad, who is back in the hospital with prostate and bladder infections. My mom is grieving and worried about my dad. I'm her only daughter now. My sister's adult children are causing us concern because they're having trouble letting go. And now my husband is being difficult."

- Injured need(s): Competence, Autonomy, Relatedness

COACH:

"You've got a lot going on, Client. With so many emotional obstacles, I'm impressed that you still remember to weigh in. It sounds like your grief has lessened with time, but not as much for your mom and your sister's children. You care about a lot of people, Client; in what ways is your husband being difficult?"

- Plausible Harmonic Group influence: Rational Competency

REVISION:

[Silence to provide space and time for the client to continue.]

"What track would you like to be on, Client?"

- ICF Coaching Competencies: Listens Actively, Maintains Presence, Evokes Awareness, Embodies a Coaching Mindset, Cultivates Trust and Safety

EXAMPLE 7: TRAUMATIC LOSS, INCARCERATION

CLIENT:

"A little history; I was a teen mom to a little preemie girl. I already had a one-year-old when my preemie daughter was born and had a third baby before she died. Her death was deemed malnutrition, and the baby's father and I received a second-degree murder charge. At the time, I was eighteen with two other young kids, and I went to jail for three months after burying my baby girl. It's been nearly thirty years, but I still can't visit her grave. I've married and divorced two abusive husbands. Now, I live with PTSD and fibromyalgia. Life has been a struggle, but I make the most of it."

- Injured need(s): Autonomy, Competence, Relatedness

COACH:

"Wow! You've overcome a lot, Client. You've had many obstacles, and I see why your life feels like a struggle. I can't imagine what it would be like to lose a child, let alone go to jail for it. How did you survive all of that? You're obviously a resilient and strong person, Client, I admire that. Do you currently or have you ever worked with a counselor?"

- Plausible Harmonic Group influence: Emotional Realness

REVISION:

"Thank you for your transparency, Client. What's important for me to understand about you related to our work together?"

- ICF Coaching Competencies: Establishes and Maintains Agreements, Listens Actively, Embodies a Coaching Mindset, Evokes Awareness, Cultivates Trust and Safety, Maintains Presence

EXAMPLE 8: ADDICTION

CLIENT:

"I want to learn not to be controlling. My son, an addict, will go to treatment soon, and I know I sometimes get overbearing. I run on a treadmill to relieve some of my anxiety, but I want to learn to be more patient with my son. When he gets back from treatment, I want to be understanding instead of judgemental."

- Injured need(s): Competence, Relatedness

COACH:

"It sounds like you've got a lot of stress, Client. I'm glad you're running for your physical and mental health; that's important with so much going on in your life. What about sleep and nutrition? How are those areas of your life? In the past, when have you felt successful in setting aside the judgment and practicing patience?"

- Plausible Harmonic Group influence: Rational Competency

REVISION:

"How will you know when you've achieved more patience and understanding, Client?"

- ICF Coaching Competencies: Evokes Awareness, Maintains Presence, Listens Actively, Embodies a Coaching Mindset, Cultivates Trust and Safety

EXAMPLE 9: DEATH

CLIENT:

"My best friend's dad passed away yesterday after ten years with Alzheimer's. He took a turn for the worse a few weeks ago and passed pretty suddenly. He was one of those people who felt like a dad to everyone who knew him."

- Injured need(s): Relatedness

COACH:

"So sorry for your loss. My sympathy to you."

- Plausible Harmonic Group influence: Rational Competency, Positive Outlook

REVISION:

[Silence to provide space and time for the client to continue.]

"What are you feeling as you share that with me, Client?"

- ICF Coaching Competencies: Cultivates Trust and Safety, Evokes Awareness, Listens Actively, Embodies a Coaching Mindset, Maintains Presence

EXAMPLE 10: CHILDHOOD TRAUMA

CLIENT:

"I want to tell you right up front that a lot of my issues are due to childhood sexual abuse. Because of how messed up my childhood was, I learned to soothe myself with food, so now I'm obese and try to learn healthier eating habits, but it's not easy because I love sweets."

- Injured need(s): Competence, Autonomy

COACH:

"I appreciate your openness and honesty in sharing that with me, Client. I hope this space continues to be a safe place for you to share whatever is on your mind. The mind can be a dangerous space when the past interferes with the present. I'm wondering if you have a counselor to talk with about these things so that you can focus on this program while you're here?"

- Plausible Harmonic Group influence: Rational Competency, Emotional Realness

REVISION:

"What makes healthier eating habits important to you, Client?"

- ICF Coaching Competencies: Embodies a Coaching Mindset, Evokes Awareness, Maintains Presence, Cultivates Trust and Safety, Listens Actively

EXAMPLE 11: EMPTY NESTER

CLIENT:

"I didn't finish my goal because my son left for college over the weekend. That was harder than I thought."

- Injured need(s): Relatedness, Competence

COACH:

"Oh, yeah, it's like when you send your last child to kindergarten, isn't it? I had a horrible time when my youngest moved out. It can be hard to stick with healthy intentions when faced with emotional upheavals! So I'm curious, what went well this weekend?"

- Plausible Harmonic Group influence: Emotional Realness, Positive Outlook

REVISION:

"What made it harder than you thought, Client?"

- ICF Coaching Competencies: Embodies a Coaching Mindset, Listens Actively, Cultivates Trust and Safety, Evokes Awareness, Maintains Presence

EXAMPLE 12: JOB LOSS

CLIENT:

"I lost my job, so I don't know how long I can keep talking to you."

- Injured need(s): Competence, Relatedness, Autonomy

COACH:

"Oh, no! I'm sorry to hear about your job, Client. Do you have another job lined up? I'm sure our support department can tell you if this benefit continues when your position ends. Here's a direct phone number so they can give you a definitive answer."

- Plausible Harmonic Group influence: Positive Outlook, Emotional Realness, Rational Competency

REVISION:

"What's coming up for you as you tell me that, Client?"

- ICF Coaching Competencies: Embodies a Coaching Mindset, Maintains Presence, Evokes Awareness, Listens Actively, Cultivates Trust and Safety

EXAMPLE 13: LOSS OF TRADITIONS

CLIENT:

"I missed out on my college graduation ceremony because of Covid."

- Injured need(s): Relatedness, Autonomy, Competence

COACH:

"Yeah, 2020 was an awful year for students of all ages. I'm sorry you missed out on your graduation ceremony, Client. I know some kids didn't mind the absence of end-of-year celebrations, but hear that you aren't one of them. So what were you able to do in place of a graduation ceremony?"

- Plausible Harmonic Group influence: Positive Outlook, Emotional Realness

REVISION:

"What does missing out on graduation mean to you, Client?"

- ICF Coaching Competencies: Embodies a Coaching Mindset, Maintains Presence, Listens Actively, Cultivates Trust and Safety, Evokes Awareness

EXAMPLE 14: CHRONIC ILLNESS

CLIENT:

"I found out last Sunday that a dear aunt received an Alzheimer's diagnosis recently. Unfortunately, she has to undergo a spinal tap to determine the extent of the illness next month."

- Injured need(s): Relatedness, Competence

COACH:

"What a terrible, awful disease. I'm so sorry for this heartbreaking news. How is your aunt taking it? How are you?"

- Plausible Harmonic Group influence: Emotional Realness

REVISION:

"How is this news hitting you, Client?"

- ICF Coaching Competencies: Embodies a Coaching Mindset, Maintains Presence, Evokes Awareness, Listens Actively, Cultivates Trust and Safety

EXAMPLE 15: TRAUMATIC LOSS, WEIGHT LOSS

CLIENT:

"I want to take control of my health. Along with this program, I sought counseling at the beginning of the year to learn to care for myself and my health again. Twelve years ago I lost 150 lbs. Eleven yrs ago we lost my daughter and my mother, both from different illnesses, three months apart. I finally feel like I can start to make changes in my life for myself, but its a jerky process. Lots of starts and stalls. I will do better, in terms of weight loss, as well as mentally, it just may be slower than expected. But, I won't give up."

- Injured need(s): Competence, Relatedness, Autonomy

COACH:

"Thank you for sharing all of this background information with me, Client, it helps me to help you. You've been through a lot and it sounds like you're ready to get back on the horse! Also, congratulations on your weight loss! That's no small accomplishment and says a lot about your tenacity. As we get started together, what does your current weight loss plan look like?"

- Plausible Harmonic Group influence: Positive Outlook, Rational Competency, Emotional Realness

REVISION:

"What's it like to feel ready to make yourself a priority, Client?"

- ICF Coaching Competencies: Embodies a Coaching Mindset, Evokes Awareness, Listens Actively, Maintains Presence, Cultivates Trust and Safety

EXAMPLE 16: PET LOSS

CLIENT:

"I can't seem to get back on track since my chinchilla, Harry, died."

- Injured need(s): Relatedness, Competence

COACH:

"Oh, boy, losing a pet is horrible; I'm sorry you had to experience that. A chinchilla, you say?! How long do chinchilla's typically live? How did he die?"

- Plausible Harmonic Group influence: Positive Outlook, Emotional Realness

REVISION:

"What track would you like to be on, Client?"

- ICF Coaching Competencies: Embodies a Coaching Mindset, Cultivates Trust and Safety, Evokes Awareness, Listens Actively, Maintains Presence

EXAMPLE 17: TRAUMATIC LOSS

CLIENT:

"I don't care what people say about my boy. Let them judge while their kids are alive. Yeah, he was on the corner selling drugs when he was shot, but what he was doing doesn't make it right."

- Injured need(s): Relatedness, Competence

COACH:

"People are cruel, Client. I can hear how much your son meant to you and how misunderstood and angry you feel. It's hard for me to imagine what you must go through everyday. How long ago did it happen?"

- Plausible Harmonic Group influence: Emotional Realness

REVISION:

"I notice substantial energy as you say that, Client. What feelings are beneath that energy?"

- ICF Coaching Competencies: Cultivates Trust and Safety, Maintains Presence, Embodies a Coaching Mindset, Evokes Awareness, Listens Actively

EXAMPLE 18: MARITAL STRIFE

CLIENT:

"My husband told me last night that he wants to leave me because he says I'm a downer. I was molested from the age of five until I was twelve years old; I'm forty-five now, and I can still smell him. I don't mean to be negative, and I don't know what to do."

- Injured need(s): Competence, Autonomy, Relatedness

COACH:

"Thank you for your transparency, Client. It sounds like your childhood greatly impacted you. How long have you been married? Did your husband know about the abuse before you were married?"

- Plausible Harmonic Group influence: Rational Competency, Emotional Realness

REVISION:

[Silence to provide space and time for the client to continue.]

"What would be most helpful to accomplish during our call today, Client?"

- ICF Coaching Competencies: Establishes and Maintains Agreements, Maintains Presence, Listens Actively, Embodies a Coaching Mindset, Cultivates Trust and Safety

EXAMPLE 19: WORK/LIFE BALANCE

CLIENT:

"My daughter has surgery next week. When she's in the hospital, I'll work while I'm there because I'm just really sitting there waiting for her to get discharged, so it keeps my mind occupied."

- Injured need(s): Competence, Relatedness

COACH:

"Sure, sure, that's understandable. Is there anything else you feel you're really needing for this month that you're wanting to focus on to help you manage?"

- Plausible Harmonic Group influence: Rational Competency

REVISION:

"What happens if you don't keep your mind occupied, Client?"

- ICF Coaching Competencies: Embodies a Coaching Mindset, Maintains Presence, Listens Actively, Evokes Awareness, Cultivates Trust and Safety

EXAMPLE 20: DELIVERING A DEATH NOTIFICATION

CLIENT:

"I was tasked with telling a mother that her son died this week. No one wants this duty: it's like getting the short end of the stick. I can't help imagining how I would feel if a police officer came to my door to tell me my child had died. You never forget the screams."

- Injured need(s): Autonomy, Relatedness

COACH:

"I can't imagine what that must be like for you, Client. It must take a lot of courage and resolve just to knock on the door. That mother was lucky to have a compassionate officer give her such awful news."

- Plausible Harmonic Group influence: Positive Outlook

REVISION:

"How do these conversations impact you, Client?"

- ICF Coaching Competencies: Evokes Awareness, Embodies a Coaching Mindset, Maintains Presence, Cultivates Trust and Safety, Listens Actively

EXAMPLE 21: TRAUMATIC LOSS

CLIENT:

"When I was eighteen years old, I got pregnant. My parents were more than disappointed in me; they were ashamed of me. They kicked me out of the house and out of the small town we lived in. I moved in with some friends near my college and decided to give the baby up for adoption. The pregnancy went well, and I chose a family that would adopt my baby girl immediately after delivery. The delivery went fine, no complications or anything, I mean. Then my baby girl was born dead. She was dead inside me. I had an ultrasound the week before, and she was healthy, and then she was dead. I tried to do right by her, and she never had a chance."

- Injured need(s): Relatedness, Autonomy, Competence

COACH:

"What an awful experience, Client. I hear that you were resourceful and compassionate in making such a mature decision. I can't imagine having the courage to give up a baby. How did you move forward from such grief?"

- Plausible Harmonic Group influence: Positive Outlook, Emotional Realness

REVISION:

"How did that experience shape who you are today, Client?"

- ICF Coaching Competencies: Cultivates Trust and Safety, Maintains Presence, Listens Actively, Evokes Awareness, Embodies a Coaching Mindset

EXAMPLE 22: TRAUMATIC LOSS

CLIENT:

"So get this; my cousin, who is thirty-one years old had a fight with his girlfriend, and they were together for a long time but they broke up. A couple of days later, my cousin hung himself. Then his girlfriend found out that he died and how he died, and she hung herself. They both died that way. They both died."

- Injured need(s): Relatedness, Competence

COACH:

"Oh my gosh, Client! How awful! I can't imagine how you must be feeling. Were you close to your cousin? Or his girlfriend? When did it happen?"

- Plausible Harmonic Group influence: Emotional Realness

REVISION:

[Silence to provide space and time for the client to continue.]

"What are you experiencing as you retell this story to me, Client?"

- ICF Coaching Competencies: Embodies a Coaching Mindset, Maintains Presence, Evokes Awareness, Listens Actively, Cultivates Trust and Safety

EXAMPLE 23: DISCRIMINATION

CLIENT:

"As per usual over the past 17 years, I went to the home office for a nurse's meeting. As I was walking in, by myself and with my ID card on a lanyard right in full view, a woman walked up to me, blocking my entry and asked why I was there. Mind you, while I was stopped, four other white women walked right past us and no one stopped them. They walked right into the meeting along with several other white people. It took me a while to connect the dots of what changed my mood that day, but that was it. It's humiliating and disappointing that this shit continues to happen. It would be nice if I wasn't singled out for not having white skin during my lifetime. But I doubt that'll happen."

- Injured need(s): Relatedness, Autonomy, Competence

COACH:

"That sounds horrible, Client. I'm sorry that happened to you. Did you confront the woman who stopped you? I'd like to give her a piece of my mind!"

- Plausible Harmonic Group influence: Emotional Realness

REVISION:

[Silence to provide space and time for the client to continue.]

"What's your belief about yourself in this situation, Client?"

- ICF Coaching Competencies: Embodies a Coaching Mindset, Maintains Presence, Evokes Awareness, Listens Actively, Cultivates Trust and Safety

EXAMPLE 24: TRAUMATIC LOSS

HOLLY:

"Half an hour before my son's party, my dad collapsed and was rushed to the hospital, unconscious. I had just spoken to him; he was en route to our house. I dropped everything and headed to the hospital, without knowing many details. I called all three of my boys to tell them what I knew and arranged rides to the hospital for them all. I asked friends to clean up the party preparations and tell people that came by what happened.

I waited to hear any news at the hospital after being shuffled into a private room. Eventually, a nurse came and asked me if I wanted to be with him. I didn't know what she was talking about, but I said yes and followed her out.

While on the way to the ER, I remember telling myself that I would walk in there and tell him to "just get the fuck up." As they pulled back the curtain, revealing my father with some machine on his chest and a tube down his throat, I screamed and squatted to the floor.

I tried to rise and see my dad, but all I could do was look and scream and duck down again. Over and over. A doctor followed me up and down, telling me that they tried to revive him for ninety minutes, which is the maximum time for this procedure. She wanted me to know that when they stopped it, he would be dead. Or something like that.

Mostly, I was thinking, 'He's not coming out of this, he's not coming out of this. My dad is gone. What?' And then I knew I had to hold his hand as they turned off the machine keeping his body alive. I had to. I couldn't let him be alone at that moment. I had to smell him one more time.

I was having a graduation party for my son. How did I get here? What did I need to do next? I had to tell people. So, first, I called my son, Nicholas, who was not having his party that day."

- Injured need(s): Relatedness, Competence, Autonomy

COACH:

"I want to offer my condolences. Thank you for sharing this story with me. That must have been so hard to manage at the time. Losing a dad is never easy, even when it's expected, let alone unexpected. Was it a heart attack? Your sons must be devastated. Were you able to reschedule your son's party?"

- Plausible Harmonic Group influence: Emotional Realness, Rational Competency

REVISION:

[Silence to provide space and time for the client to continue.]

"What comes up for you when you share that story with me, Client?"

- ICF Coaching Competencies: Cultivates Trust and Safety, Maintains Presence, Listens Actively, Embodies a Coaching Mindset, Evokes Awareness

LIVING WITH GRIEF: DAY 160, NOWHERE

I read this word recently, and I saw it differently than intended. Or did I?

Nowhere.

Now here.

Nowhere is how I feel when grief takes over. It is where despair binds and tortures me. I am here, and I can't get away.

Nowhere.

No. Where?

Nowhere is how I feel to get through a day. I am an empty shell.

Nowhere is where you'll find my feelings of happiness and contentment.

Nowhere can I find my dad and my son.

Nowhere is the cruelest game of hide-and-seek ever.

IN CLOSING

Coaches often get into this line of work to "help" others, yet often we don't recognize how we obstruct the coaching relationship without self-awareness and self-regulation. In truth, our attempts to help might be more about meeting our needs than our clients' needs. But how do we know the difference?

The short answer is courageous self-observation. However, laughably, most humans believe themselves more evolved and insightful than they are, demonstrating the improbability of seeing ourselves accurately.

Concurrently, most humans fear death, making grief and mortality frenetically avoided topics, which makes addressing them equally unpopular.

So, how can coaches coach on topics they avoid, deny, and fear?

Our personality (ego) and its *dominant bias* are too sophisticated for us to see through easily. Like our clients, we need another human being to mirror us and our foibles.

CLOSING INQUIRIES

This book's call-to-action is recognizing that it takes peeling back the layers of you, like an onion, to *be with* your clients rather than *doing* coaching to them. What do I mean by that? On the outside, we have the title of coach. Some have lots of coach training, and others have zero. Yet, beneath all the layers of education, training, and experience—the things we *learn to do*—is *who we are*. When we're comfortable with and confident in *ourselves* and our skills, we don't need to work so hard to coach.

- What moves you toward something and away from something else?
- How do attractions and aversions impact your coaching?
- Like the *Wizard of Oz*, what self-seeking motives lurk behind your curtain?

"Every loss has meaning, and all losses are to be grieved—
and witnessed. I have a rule on pet loss.
'If the love is real, the grief is real.'
The grief that comes with loss is how we experience the depths
of our love, and love takes many forms in this life."

— David Kessler, *Finding Meaning*

CHAPTER TEN

BEYOND THE SHOCK POINT

"If each of us could truly see and connect with the humanity of the person in front of us, search for that key that opens the door to whatever we may have in common, whether cosplay or Star Trek or the loss of a parent, it could begin to affect how we see the world and others in it."

— Isabel Wilkerson, *Caste: The Origins of Our Discontents*

MEANING AND A SENSE OF PURPOSE

I suspect that most of us who fall in love with coaching feel some sense of purpose or meaning behind the passion. Likewise, several of us have read Victor Frankl's book, *Man's Search for Meaning*, and appreciate the potency of inherent value and feeling a personal sense of purpose. For those of you that haven't read it, here's a very brief synopsis in my words:

While in concentration camps during WWII, Frankl observed the resilience of prisoners who believed that a loved one outside of the camp waited for their release. These prisoners, who embraced hope while suffering, survived the horrific Auschwitz concentration camps. Conversely, the prisoners who thought no one waited for them outside of the camps felt little hope and, thus, no reason to survive their pain—and they often didn't.

A coach's takeaway from Frankl's work: Feeling a sense of purpose and finding meaning in one's existence is integral in the coaching context from both the coach's and client's perspectives.

YOU

Let's explore this perspective beginning with you, the coach.

I feel confident that you can recognize a sense of loss in your life when it occurs. And yet, I suspect that there are experiences that you may not perceive as grief-producing, though a loss may be present. Consider, for instance, how it feels for you when a client decides to cease coaching; not only do you now have a hole in your schedule, you have less income, and one less professional relationship. The cessation of a coaching relationship is one place anxiety and our inner critic may enter the picture.

PAUSE AND REFLECT:

Most of us didn't get into coaching because we derive a charge from chasing after potential clients, so what drives us? What keeps you from giving up when you lose a client?

To answer this question, you might consider what drew you to coaching and the meaning it holds for you. For example, how do you feel when a client has an 'aha' moment in your presence? Isn't it awe-inspiring to witness the lightbulb and subsequent hope alight a client's face when they find an answer themselves? Likewise, supporting and experiencing the energy generated for change is awe-inspiring. And I imagine you feel a similar honor as me in providing a safe space to hold another's vulnerability and witness them achieve desired personal outcomes.

In what ways does coaching fulfill a sense of purpose and meaning for you?

YOUR CLIENT

Next, let's look at how a sense of purpose might impact our clients. Whether a new client seeks coaching because they've recently experienced trauma or loss, or an existing client has a loss or traumatic experience during your coaching relationship, be curious about what gives their life meaning and how that fits into their everyday experience.

Events like the death of an elderly grandparent or a friend with stage four cancer may not be unexpected, but expectation does not diminish sorrow; it merely provides logical sense. Likewise, events like infidelity, learning about one's parent's impending divorce, or a family member going to jail will jostle one's worldview and cause doubt in what was once a stable and trusted relationship. Additionally, some experiences are so traumatic that your client may question or doubt their life and security in this world, such as a child's death, a violent accident, or sexual assault (their own or a loved one).

If the trauma was not long ago, your client might be in shock. Therapy may be optimal, and you should recommend it if it seems appropriate. However, remember that you have a place in their care, too, as a witness. Witnessing includes creating a safe space capable of holding any emotion while upholding professional boundaries. It's demonstrating courage without drama and often with few words. Witnessing is staying consciously present to your client's feelings, not their story and not your story. And it offers unwavering stability so your client can find the grounding to stumble upon hope and meaning again.

BEING WITNESSED AFTER NICHOLAS' DEATH

While I heard endless platitudes after Nicholas died, pockets of interactions felt genuine and personal. These people I interacted with intended to comfort me, not tell me about themselves (i.e., I'm sorry for your loss, I can't imagine what you're going through). These people weren't afraid of my tragedy or could still witness it if they were fearful of it. I would like to share these moments to demonstrate the simplicity of meaningful responsiveness.

- A simple message after learning of Nicholas' death:
  - "Love you." (this was it, nothing more to the note.)

- When a friend heard the news of Nicholas' death:
  - Her text to me; "Oh fuck, Holly."

- An emotionally triggered moment of mine:
  - My friend took a deep breath, put her hand on my arm, and sat in silence with me until the moment passed.

- On my first day back to work (two weeks after Nicholas died):
  - I walked in the door and began crying, and a compassionate friend kept me from collapsing (literally) with a bear hug and few words.

- In another of my emotionally triggered moments:
  - My friend put a hand on my arm, gave me a warm glance, and waited in silence until it passed.

- A text message in the days after Nicholas' death:
  - "Oh my gosh, Holly. Let me buy you lunch, and you can tell me all about him."

- Seeing my physician for the first time after Nicholas' death (she also knew Nicholas, which made for more potent sorrow):
  - She gave a kind glance, took a deep breath, and offered silence while waiting for my sobs to subside.

- Nicholas' school counselor, when he approached me during the funeral:
  - He said nothing but took my hand and looked at me with compassion for just a moment. Then he was gone.
- A random text from a friend three years after Nicholas' death:
  - "I thought of Nicholas today."
- Encountering a friend who knew Nicholas in a store nearly three years after his death:
  - She looked me in the eye while discussing the specifics of his death (she is an expert in the field). Yet amid an earthshattering topic, she was welcoming and confident and offered a hug that was strong enough to hold my grief.
- From a friend and colleague while writing this book:
  - "Sending you love and aloha dear woman and congrats again on the book. What a wonderful tribute for your son. I remember him very well…I hope you are doing okay."

PAUSE AND REFLECT:

- How did these responses impact you?
- After learning about the Enneagram's dominant biases, have you found one that feels familiar?
- If so, how does your dominant bias impact your ability to witness without trying to comfort, change, improve, or fix your clients?

CONSIDER THIS:

There were no platitudes, fear, a changing of the subject, an attempt to fix or change, nor emotional expression or withdrawal. Instead, these people were present with me and my pain when it was happening and willing to move forward with me in *my* time. Their courage, patience, compassion, and empathy never waivered. These folks did one small but impactful thing, sometimes without words, which offered unsung hope.

These people became sources of strength because they could withstand my intense desperation without muddying it with an emotion of their own. They did not try to share my grief nor alter it; instead, they witnessed it.

Some coaches hope to say the right thing when a client shares a tragedy. They want their clients to thrive, not languish. However, it's not a coach's role to improve anything for their clients. Coaches need to witness their clients, not transform them. Transformation is always the client's job.

TISSUE?

An intriguing topic. Unbeknownst to many, offering an unrequested* tissue is not benevolent. If we are honest, we do it to assuage our own discomfort in a moment of uncertainty. Though it's socially "normal" to offer a tissue to a crying person, reaching for tissue breaks the flow of emotional energy between the griever and you. It rescues the observer but interrupts the griever's present experience. It unwittingly sends an unspoken message to the griever that it's time to stop crying.

* Please notice I said unrequested – should your client request a tissue, don't deny them. But, again, the point is to follow your client's lead rather than doing what makes you feel more comfortable.

PAUSE AND REFLECT:

- How well do you tolerate tears and snot running down your client's face?
- What questions do you ask to help your clients uncover their sense of purpose?
- How will you use everything you've learned in this book going forward?

MOVING FORWARD WITH GRIEF

When our clients experience us as calm, relaxed, curious, and compassionate, we invite all emotions to our conversation, including grief, loss, and trauma. We accept and appreciate our clients for who and where they are at that moment. We honor them and welcome their truth. Presence is not merely sharing space with your client; presence is your attention to them and their experiences. Presence is an ongoing choice on the coach's part.

Observing your thoughts as they occur is consciousness, our human capacity for active presence. As does anything we do consistently, a steady presence practice creates new neural pathways, just as consistent strength training (practice) results in power, strength, and hypertrophy. Our bodies and minds physiologically adapt to that which we ask of them. With practice (training), presence requires less effort to attain and maintain, much like becoming stronger by increasing the time and volume of weight lifted. And like most practices, what you put into it is what you get out of it.

Adhere to a consistent, active centering practice—make a schedule. Give yourself time to build a relationship with your inner witness. A sports coach expects consistency from their athlete for development and improvement, and a student practicing presence must create a consistent presence or centering practice. Likewise, a strength coach creates a training plan keeping the athlete's current physical condition in mind. Accordingly, you will begin a centering practice, bearing in mind your current level of mindful development.

Suppose you're new to a centering or presence practice; in that case, you might start with two minutes of noticing your thoughts (get acquainted with your inner witness) in a quiet space at the same time each day for a few weeks. Then, when you find yourself able to sit for a more extended period, incrementally increase the duration. There's no prescription except to commit, even when it feels useless (like when you practice doing an unassisted pullup and can only pull yourself up an inch). Do it anyway! Set aside time each day to breathe into your belly, heart, and head—being with your Centers of Intelligence. Should you be carried away with thoughts or feelings, practice noticing, letting them go, and returning to your practice.

AFTER THE SHOCK

Over time, we assimilate grief – we do not get over or past it. Where we were once an entire house with grief so dense it oozed from every window and under every door, we might have one moderate-sized room containing our suffering with an entry and exit for which we hold the key. We cannot remove, erase, or deny the room exists; it becomes a permanent addition to our refurbished home.

The life-changing nature of trauma and grief brings reevaluation of priorities. And according to Richard Tedeschi, Jane Shakespeare-Finch, Kanako Taku, and Lawrence Calhoun, *posttraumatic growth is possible through purposeful recollection of painful memories within a safe relationship.*

Through narration, space grows between experience and feelings, and we learn that loss illuminates life's delicate and precious nature. Over time, inviting clients to explore and reframe their assumptions about life and suffering through powerful inquiries allows them to create a new inner-landscape (redecorating their home).

There is no off button for the griever and the traumatized. Consequently, they can feel isolated, caught in endless loops of unwanted and sometimes horrific thoughts and memories, and few people willing to listen. However, there is safeness and relief when humanity arrives with strength enough to remain present with the griever's unceasing narratives. Where responsiveness exists and distress and despair are welcome, hope can bloom in the griever's heart.

Remember, there is no timeline for grief, and the more your client objectively retells their story, the closer they are to assimilation and posttraumatic growth. Stay responsive and courageous in your client's midst, offer no advice or wisdom; be present and radically empathic, listen, and manage your emotional reactions. Demonstrate to your clients that you can bear any topic in service of their future potential.

Remarkably, enhanced emotional growth and wisdom manifest for those living with the contrast of life before and after a traumatic experience. Traumatized folks find a new sense of purpose; they discover new meaning in their lives. With presence, responsiveness, and powerful inquiry, coaches can gently invite their clients to contemplate grief's role in their future selves. Coaches can support the sense of purpose that generates wisdom in their traumatized and grieving clients.

SELF-DEVELOPMENT AND INVITING HOPE

Hopefully, we all know that the coaching relationship includes exploring the entire person and not their presenting issue. Coaching encompasses a complete human being, not just weight loss, quitting smoking, or bettering job performance. We, coaches, get to support the unveiling of our client's values, strengths, and motivation by asking things like, "what makes this important to you?" and "how will making this change impact your future?" When our client tells us, "I want to fit into my skinny jeans," "I'll get a break on my insurance if I kick this habit," or "I want to earn more money," we know that coaching is the discovery of the whole person.

So who is the whole person when our client arrives with a story of grief, trauma, or loss? How will you get to know this entire grieving person? If the wound is fresh, set aside hopes of 'aha' moments and goal setting. Instead, when listening to narratives of grief and trauma, reserve your standard coaching methods for another time and be consciously present.

With presence, objectivity, thoughtful inquiry, and hope, we demonstrate that our clients are more than what's happened to them. They are more than what's left after a loss – our client's experiences do not define them. Our clients don't require rescuing or resolution; they need mirroring; they look for hope in our eyes.

SELF-DISCLOSURE?

What about self-disclosure within the coaching conversation? According to the book *Posttraumatic Growth: Theory, Research, and Applications* by Richard Tedeschi, Jane Shakespeare-Finch, Kanako Taku, and Lawrence Calhoun, *"Those who not only disclosed their stressful experiences but also perceived their recipients' reactions as involving mutual disclosure reported a higher level of posttraumatic growth than those who experienced negative reactions to their disclosures."*

When coaches practice conscious presence and self-regulation, sharing a similar experience while maintaining coaching presence and professional boundaries supports our client's growth potential through our shared humanity. How does objective and appropriate disclosure support the client's development? Our vulnerability mirrors hope and the possibility of living despite suffering.

I know the high stakes of grief and vulnerability, so I'm willing to share my losses with others experiencing similar sorrow. I do so without fanfare or emotion, keeping the client center stage. Yet, I validate their grief through my vulnerability, revealing our shared humanity.

A client sent me the following passage after I shared the basics of my losses with her. In her first correspondence, she shared her story of losing both daughter and mother within a few months. She felt the gravity of her losses on her health and wanted me to have the entire picture. Immediately, the impact of appropriate self-disclosure is evident.

"You were so smart to seek counseling from the beginning. I appreciate and am thankful for your willingness to share with me your grief. It does help to know that you understand. I normally don't share my loss with anyone. I'm sure you're familiar with the way the loss of a child makes others so uncomfortable. I feel like physical health and mental health are intertwined, and I thought that you should be aware of the mental/emotional side."

LIVING WITH GRIEF: DAY 274, SINCE-THEN-TIME

My Since-Then-Time has been 274 days long. LONG.

You know those nightmares that are so real you can't tell it's a nightmare until you wake up, and then you feel so relieved that it was just a nightmare? Well, my life is the opposite. One night I dreamed Nicholas was back; he was with me. I was aware that it was a miracle that I had him back. And then, I woke up.

My nightmare begins every day when I remember my son is dead.

My therapist tells me that two realities are battling in my mind, and I'm trying to learn to hold them both at once: I am alive, and my son is not. It's most challenging to have them both simultaneously.

And yet, here I am. I am here.

I portion my energy and avoid haste. I used to thrive on having many places to be and lots of things to do, but I don't anymore. I have a new stress threshold, and I won't overschedule or do something that I don't want to do. I can't. I'm establishing a Since-Then-Time routine that includes prioritizing what I value, which I do with deliberate and unintentional slowness.

Deliberate. Intentional. Great descriptions of how things get done slowly now because I choose to go down a rabbit hole that has caught my attention. How often are we intentional, and how often are we asleep with our eyes open? If we sleep through reality, it's simple to blame, redirect, rationalize, and justify our behaviors. It's also easier to have regrets.

Everything seems intentional these days. And at the same time not. I have to talk myself into entering the world every day because it's fraught with pain. So I wonder, does being intentional equal being present, or is it more connected to endurance?

I used to think endurance was about physical stamina. I admired Ironman athletes. I don't doubt it takes strength and determination to complete a 2.4-mile swim, 112-mile bike ride, and a marathon all rolled up in one, but I can tell you that I would do one Ironman each month for the rest of my life if I could have my son back. I would gladly take the grueling physical pain and long-term overuse injuries over the boundless despair accompanying losing a child for good.

Now, I can see that my life has diminished into a perpetual endurance event.

Where is my finish line, I ask? My endurance event has a timer that runs on a continuous loop with no finish line.

Somehow, during the first year after losing a child, the mind of a grieving mother clings to the hope that she can do something to change the outcome; she can see what went wrong and can go back and remove the threat so her child can live and life can go on. It may sound ridiculous, but it's true. It is a predictable stage that grieving mothers undergo.

And then time goes by, and the nightmare remains her reality.

IN CLOSING

Life is full of transitions that don't include trauma yet require us to change something fundamental about ourselves. Even when we perceive a change as an improvement, leaving something behind affects who we are.

For instance, whether planned or not, having a child is a critical moment in a person's life that includes the loss of autonomy. Similarly, moving out of a parent's home is often an enormous shock point for both child and parent, though, at that moment, the child probably doesn't recognize it as anything but exciting. Additionally, leaving one job for another can be a significant transition even when we perceive it as a wise or fortunate move. Lastly, writing and publishing a book is an immense undertaking; at publishing, one is likely not the same person that wrote the first sentence.

Transformation takes fortitude, *conscious presence*, inner witnessing, consistency, and seeing ourselves mirrored in another's eyes. So, where do you stand on your self-development, Coach? Will you continue to learn more about your Enneagram dominant bias and Harmonic Group? Are you curious about how your dominant bias impacts your coaching and life? If so, you'll need others who are a bit farther down that road to mirror what's possible—perhaps a certified Enneagram coach or community of your own is worth considering.

In that case, the following links will bring you to reputable resources that offer Enneagram insights and tests and one that allows you to search for an Accredited Enneagram Professional. And check out the Appendix for additional reading opportunities.

The Narrative Enneagram:

https://www.narrativeenneagram.org/

The Enneagram Institute:

https://www.enneagraminstitute.com/

The International Enneagram Association:

https://www.internationalenneagram.org/

CLOSING INQUIRIES

One last thought for coaches; self-efficacy is a critical component of maintaining our capacity for conscious presence with our clients while avoiding burnout. Self-efficacy is not the number of trophies, diplomas, certifications, or degrees we hold. Nor is it a personality ruse affirming our impact, peace, rectitude, connections, achievements, uniqueness, prowess, certitude, or gratification.

Instead, self-efficacy is the benevolence, engagement, flexibility, humility, authenticity, equanimity, clarity, courage, and gratitude you see mirrored in your client's eyes.

- What gives your life purpose, Coach?
- Who are you in your client's eyes?
- What stood out to you in this book?

"Sorry. Everyone told her they were sorry. Why didn't they tell her how to go on living instead? How to keep going day after day when soon it was going to be a year since she buried Lucy and Francis. Then two years, then three. Why did no one tell her how to keep living?"

— Kate Quinn, *The Rose Code*

YOU CAN DO MORE THAN IMAGINE

*"Nobody wants to talk about it. Nobody wants to acknowledge or
remember. It's like a scab that gets better and shrinks,
but it's always there. It's always a part of you.
It's like growing an extra finger; sometimes people notice it,
sometimes they don't. Sometimes you can hide it;
sometimes, you can't. But, it's never gone;
it'll be with you until the day you die."*

— Joanne Grimsrud

A MOVING TARGET

By now, you have a sense of how important it is to know yourself as expertly as possible while dancing with the shenanigans of your personality and its dominant biases and Harmonic Group defenses. We've stood bravely removing our masks in the service of authenticity and transparency with our tender-hearted clients, yet, somehow, we still freeze and fall to platitudes at the mention of an awful loss or tragedy.

So what might open up in a conversation when a coach stays present and confident amidst complex and often painful topics? Below you will find an ongoing conversation with a client after her daughter's death. Notice her comfort in talking about things she's learned are uncomfortable for others and her self-protective nature, knowing benevolence is not the primary motive of most people in her time of grief.

Client:

"A moving target is just how I feel. People mean well, but it is so awkward for people to approach me. First, because it's hard to know what to say to someone who just lost their child, and second because of the very public and violent way she died.

I know people are talking about it and judging her, but I don't do Facebook or read comments on any local news, so they can just piss off. The worst is having people call or text that I haven't talked to in forever. They want gory details, and I am not having any of that."

PAUSE AND REFLECT:

What does this short but emotionally powerful excerpt bring up for you? What would you say to her next?

What can you take away from this passage and apply to your work with grieving and traumatized clients?

WHAT ARE YOU AFRAID OF?

Below are the things **not** to say, nonetheless, commonly said. Though there are different variations of unhelpful and sometimes even hurtful comments, opinions, and judgments, the resonant messages and their interpreted meanings are:

I'M UNCOMFORTABLE; LET'S CHANGE THE SUBJECT.

- Don't cry.
- You will feel happiness again.
- Don't be sad; he's in a better place.
- Take comfort in knowing that he's not suffering.
- Time heals all wounds.
- I'm sorry.
- I can't imagine what you're going through.
- My condolences.
- That's too bad.
- That's a shame.
- I will keep you in my thoughts.
- This, too, shall pass.
- How unfortunate.
- He brought this on himself.
- It must have been his time to go.
- Think of all the fun times you had together.
- Aren't you passed this yet?
- I hope you take comfort in the positive memories of him.
- My sympathy to you.
- Stop being so selfish. Let her rest in peace.
- Stop crying.
- Pull yourself together.

I KNOW WHAT'S BEST FOR YOU.

- You can't keep saying things like that (in response to hearing a wish not to live).
- You will feel happiness again.
- What are you doing to take care of yourself?
- Taking walks will help.
- Have you tried yoga?
- Aren't you overreacting?
- Think of your other children.
- Bad things happen, you have to go on.
- Be happy she's gone.
- You have to be strong for your children.
- How could you just let him die?
- What's underneath this?
- Look on the bright side.
- You have to look at the positive.
- Everything happens for a reason.
- It'll get easier.
- It'll get better.
- Nothing will ever hurt this much again. Even if one of your other children dies, it'll never hurt this much.
- I'll bring you a casserole later today.

YOU HAVE IT BETTER THAN ME.

- At least you have [two] other children.
- At least you spoke to him before he died. At least you have that.
- You can still have another child.
- At least you can have children.

I'M ALL-KNOWING.

- You know you never have to do it again when you get through this.
- The pain won't always be this bad.
- He would want you to move on and be happy.
- You had eighteen great years with him.
- You'll feel better eventually.
- Time heals all wounds.
- At least he won't suffer anymore.
- God never gives you more than you can handle.
- He was such a good person that God wanted him in Heaven with him.
- It was God's will.
- Maybe it's better this way.
- At least the grief should be easier since she was so young.
- When life gives you lemons, make lemonade.
- Think about the good things in your life.

I WANT TO KNOW THE DETAILS.

- What happened?
- How did [he] die?
- What does your grief feel like?
- Was it unexpected?
- When did it happen?
- Was it [cancer, an accident, etc.]?
- How did you lose your son?

TAKING CARE OF YOU MAKES ME FEEL BETTER.

- How can I help?
- How are you?
- What can I do?
- [He's] in a better place.
- You can get through this.
- Here's a tissue.

WHAT ABOUT ME?

- You're handling things better than I am.
- When will *you* be back?
- I miss who you used to be.
- I miss you.
- How long does grief take?
- I know how you feel.
- I lost my _____ that way, too.
- It could have been worse; my _____ died by _____.
- I wouldn't be able to get out of bed if I were you.
- I'd have to quit my job if it were me.

PAUSE AND REFLECT:

What's your experience as you read through these typical platitudes? How does seeing comments you've probably said on this list impact you, if at all?

Will you continue to use them or try something different?

Now, try out one of the above platitudes after reading again the tragic "moving target" quote. Go ahead, say it out loud.

Client:

"A moving target is just how I feel. People mean well, but it is so awkward for people to approach me. First, because it's hard to know what to say to someone who just lost their child, and second because of the very public and violent way she died.

I know people are talking about it and judging her, but I don't do Facebook or read comments on any local news, so they can just piss off. The worst is having people call or text that I haven't talked to in forever. They want gory details, and I am not having any of that."

You: (Choose from the list above)

PAUSE AND REFLECT:

What did you choose to say? What did you notice after you said your chosen reply?

What would you do differently next time, if anything?

JUST ONE UNCOMPLICATED EXPRESSION

Keep in mind that without your conscious presence, the following is mere apathy, but with presence, it can provide comfort:

After a deep, consciously centering breath, "Oh, Client."

Now try this simple, effortless response with our grieving client.

Client:

"A moving target is just how I feel. People mean well, but it is so awkward for people to approach me. First, because it's hard to know what to say to someone who just lost their child, and second because of the very public and violent way she died.

I know people are talking about it and judging her, but I don't do Facebook or read comments on any local news, so they can just piss off. The worst is having people call or text that I haven't talked to in forever. They want gory details, and I am not having any of that."

You: *After a deep, centering breath, "Oh, Client."*

How does it feel to say something so simple?

What might this simple affirmation invite?

"Happiness is beneficial for the body,
but it is grief that develops the powers of the mind."

— *Marcel Proust*

REFERENCES AND RESOURCES

"Dr. Dan Siegel Home Page - Dr. Dan Siegel." *Dr. Dan Siegel*, https://drdansiegel.com/. Accessed 23 Apr. 2022.

"Enneagram: Helen Palmer." Enneagram : Helen Palmer, http://www.enneagram.com/index.html. Accessed 23 Apr. 2022.

Frankl, Viktor E. *Man's Search for Meaning*. Beacon Press, 2014.

Hudson, Russ. *The Enneagram: Nine Gateways to Presence*. Sounds True, 2021.

Hudson, Russ and Jessica Dibb. "A Year-Long Enneagram Certification Program in Conscious Living." (April 2021 - May 2022)

Kegan, Robert. *In Over Our Heads*. Harvard University Press, 1994.

Kessler, David. *Finding Meaning*. Scribner, 2019.

Killen, Jack. *Toward the Neurobiology of the Enneagram*. The Enneagram Journal, 2009.

Palmer, Helen. *The Enneagram*. Harper Collins, 2011.

Riso, Don Richard, and Russ Hudson. *Personality Types*. Houghton Mifflin Harcourt, 1996.

Riso, Don Richard, and Russ Hudson. *The Wisdom of the Enneagram*. Bantam, 1999.

Riso, Don Richard, and Russ Hudson. *Understanding the Enneagram*. Houghton Mifflin Harcourt, 2000.

Ryan, Richard M., and Edward L. Deci. *Self-Determination Theory*. Guilford Publications, 2018.

Siegel, Daniel J. *The Mindful Brain: Reflection and Attunement in the Cultivation of Well-Being (Norton Series on Interpersonal Neurobiology)*. W. W. Norton & Company, 2007.

Tedeschi, Richard G., et al. *Posttraumatic Growth*. Routledge, 2018.

"Temperament and the Enneagram | David N. Daniels, M.D." *David N. Daniels, M.D.*, https://www.facebook.com/drdaviddaniels/, 23 Dec. 2017, https://drdaviddaniels.com/temperament-and-the-enneagram/.

Wilkerson, Isabel. *Caste (Oprah's Book Club)*. Random House, 2020.

ACKNOWLEDGMENTS

This book wouldn't exist if not for the two men I lost in 2018; my dad, Bob Margl, and my son, Nicholas Seidl. A bittersweet exchange. I miss you endlessly.

My sons Benjamin and Joey come next because I wouldn't be writing these words right now without them. Our lives forever changed in 2018, with sorrow still palpable. Yet, we are a three-way lifeline with a greater appreciation for love and grief. Gnstdltbbb, I love you.

Since writing these Acknowledgments, a small child arrived in my life and positively merits recognition, along with his mom, whom he wouldn't be here without. Baby Nicholas arrived on July 4th, 2022, demanding his independence. Thankfully, his mom, Katie, was willing to participate in his freedom by then. Decidedly having his dad, Joey's, features intermingled with the uncle's whose name he carries, Baby Nicholas brings renewed hope with his sweet, serene, and irresistible demeanor. Welcome, baby Yiyi. Nnstdltbbb, grandma loves you.

Thank you to all of Nicholas' teachers for supporting and valuing him. Nicholas was the teacher's pet *every year*, making it hard to name everyone. However, with the help of Joey and Benjamin, I've done my best to remember the names mentioned most often: Mrs. Lilja (whom all my boys loved), Mrs. Rust, Leon Rogolla, Jason Schlukebier, Kristi Boyer, Sara Young, Kelly Blomquist, and Danielle Hinrichs.

Lori Nakamura is my confidante and courageously honest partner in self-exploration. After twenty-two years of friendship, divorce, children, going back to work, and more heartache than anyone should bear, I would not be who I am today without you, Lori. Now that Bob's gone, you are my lifeline.

Matt Paar drove Nicholas, Joey, and me to Nicholas' dorm in New York on May 6, 2018, and he was here when the police officer brought the news of Nicholas' death on September 22, 2018. Matt steps up and gets things done when the chips are down. You've not only single-handedly taken care of the household, Matt, while I stayed buried in projects (like this book) to avoid grief, but you've endured an ogre since September 22, 2018. I know how fortunate I am, I'm just terrible at saying thank you. I love you.

Joanne Grimsrud is the courageous mother you met in Chapter 1 and a lifeline for me after Nicholas died. She shared her wisdom and story to help me unravel how to keep living, and she narrated her entire story to me to share with all of you. Joanne is an exemplar of hope, meaning, perseverance, and love.

My Schueller support team includes my mom, Jan, aunt Jill, and cousin Jeanne. I wouldn't be who I am today without these three watching out for me for my entire life. They all showed up when I needed them the most and stuck around when hell was all there was. Jeanne, thank you for showing up wholeheartedly and reigniting our relationship when Nicholas died; your weekly cards for an entire year were a lifesaver and I'm ever grateful to see you regularly again.

I'd also like to thank my mom's husband, Ron Green, who is a jack of all trades, publishing being one of those. He's shared his wisdom freely over the years and is ever supportive of my blogs and now this book. Indeed, he's been a source of writing inspiration.

I'm grateful to Megan MacDonald, Karla Alarcon, and Kayla Khang for loving Nicholas and being a part of my life. You are all saviors to my existence. I hope you will allow me to celebrate your joys and support your sorrows as you move forward in your lives.

Thank you to Jason Fischer of Orchids Ltd. and Bart Motes of Motes Orchids for registering orchids in honor of Nicholas—Paph. Memoria Nicholas Robert Margl and Vanda Yiyi, respectively.

Thank you to Kayla, Anna, Jenny, and Wendy for talking to me nearly weekly for months while striving for two passing recordings. I couldn't have done it without you, and I'm eternally grateful.

How does one choose the order in which to express thanks? This sucks! Imagine this a horizontal list, please, so there's no apparent descending order.

Gretchen—endless hours of conversation; some with tears, others with frustration, many with laughs, and all with love and respect, and biscotti, stalkers, stitches, ducks, and rabbits. If only we could remember the rabbits. But then again, my dear WB, we are gladly suffering fools, after all. Pat and Gerry—ceaselessly thoughtful, supportive, and generous; never a dull conversation or shortage of dogs. Lisa Hane—forever energized, authentic, and loyal. Thank you for your trust, sensitivity, and remembering Nicholas by supporting Rage Against Addiction. And Mary Longfellow—your courage, receptive authenticity, and innate wisdom are awe-inspiring. Thank you for allowing me to feel my grief and cry in your presence.

Many thanks to the very best neighbor ever, Michelle Stein, who is always willing to listen with sincere empathy, babysits furry babies at a moment's notice and has the neatest yard on the block. I appreciate your generous support over the past sixteen years, Michelle.

Thank you, Geriann Fedorowicz, for supporting me as I pretend to know how to live without my son and father. And much appreciation, Geriann, for welcoming Yiyi to join us.

Many thanks to Heather Doyle Fraser, my publisher, and dear friend. If I hadn't blindly registered for a writing class through Wellcoaches, I wouldn't be writing these acknowledgments right now. I've learned that this is an arduous process; I shudder to think what this book would say if not for Heather.

Closely on Heather's heels are Jesse Sussman, Angela Miller Barton, and Dino Marino, the designer. Jesse is my marketing guru who will get this book into your hand. Angela began as my coach concierge at Wellcoaches in 2011 and, by offering a writing class, introduced me to Heather in 2020. And Dino, his artistic talent put all of this together in a fancy package.

I met Thomas Lim while writing this book. Though he lives in Singapore, he has become a valued friend and professional comrade. Thomas has more vigor and vision than anyone I've met, and I'm lucky to be part of his growing company with Henry Toi, Thrive Consulting. Through Thomas, I had the great fortune to meet Kenneth Tan, another Singaporean professional with wisdom and kindness in spades.

I appreciate my manager and friend, Courtney Hoolihan, for her ongoing support and passion for the people on her team. Courtney sees my drive and many projects and graciously encourages me to take time off. I'm learning to take her advice, though it's a slow process.

Thank you, Fran Fisher and Erika Jackson, for your kind yet direct mentoring. Fran mentored me to MCC glory this year, and Erika is a mentor from way back. I most definitely wouldn't be the coach I am today without you both.

I offer intense appreciation to my Narrative Enneagram teachers, Helen Palmer, David Daniels, Renee Rosario, and Peter O'Hanrahan. Over several years, and through their Professional training track, they helped lay the foundation for what I know today. Menlo Park forever holds a special place in my heart.

Thank you to Russ Hudson and Jessica Dibb for the intensely fabulous *Enneagram in Conscious Living* course. I'm grateful for the wisdom, experiences, and connections forged in this year-long journey. Though it often felt like drinking from a firehose, this course elevated my awareness and provided the meaning I hoped to find.

Lastly, I offer a massive thanks to all of my personal training and coaching clients. I would never finish these acknowledgments if I named you all individually, yet it's crucial to me that you know I value you all. I learned something from every one of you; thank you for teaching me.

ABOUT THE AUTHOR

Holly Margl is a Master Certified Coach through the International Coaching Federation and holds two Professional Enneagram Certifications and Accreditation through the International Enneagram Association. She is the owner of alohacoach, LLC, founded in 2010; when she founded her coaching practice, she focused on health and wellness coaching, personal training, and triathlon coaching. Today, Holly's time is spent on anxiety and depression coaching, mentoring coaches, assessing students' coaching skills for Wellcoaches Inc, and acting as a Certified PEARLS Senior Coach with Thrive Consulting in Singapore.

Holly started her career in the helping profession by studying Alcohol and Drug Counseling at the University of Minnesota. Both coaching and the Enneagram landed in Holly's lap in 2011 while teaching at a local community college. Holly continues to take advantage of countless courses to advance her knowledge, assimilation, and application in both coaching and the Enneagram.

Holly Margl grew up and still lives in Saint Paul, Minnesota, with her sons Benjamin and Joey, partner Matt, Chow Chow, Yiyi, and three cats, Moose, George, and Mae. When not coaching or mentoring, Holly enjoys spending time with her family, running, baking, mountain biking, strength training, and has competed in multiple triathlons. Holly is a relatively new yet passionate orchid hobbyist with eighty-some orchids who share her office space creating an in-house tropical oasis. Last but not least, Holly is ready to explore being a new grandmother as she celebrates the birth of her new grandchild in July 2022 — a baby boy named Nicholas, after the uncle who left this world way before his time.

www.witnessinggrief.com

Printed in the USA
CPSIA information can be obtained
at www.ICGtesting.com
LVHW091113161223
766669LV00057B/1863